RECESSION-PROOF YOUR FINANCIAL LIFE

Nancy Dunnan

New York   Chicago   San Francisco   Lisbon   London
Madrid   Mexico City   Milan   New Delhi   San Juan   Seoul
Singapore   Sydney   Toronto

1012109

1 2 3 4 5 6 7 8 9 0   FGR/FGR   0 5 4 3 2 1 0 9

MHID   0-07-163460-6
ISBN 978-0-07-163460-1

Contents

1. Finding Your Money   1

2. Protecting Your Money: Safe Harbors   13

3. Buttoning Down: The Frugal Budget   27

4. Tapping into Your Assets: When You Run Out of Cash   51

5. Ramping Up Your Savings   67

6. Fighting Foreclosure and Higher Property Taxes   77

7. Surviving Credit Card Crunch   95

8. Managing Your Brokerage and 401(k) Accounts   113

9. Saving and Paying for College   135

10. Helping Those of a Certain Age   157

11. Anticipating the Pink Slip   169

12. Surviving the Pink Slip   181

13. Getting Work When There Is No Work   197

14. Having Fun: It's Chic to Be Cheap   215

    Recession Punch   225

    Index   227

1

Finding Your Money

"A fool and his money are soon parted."
—THOMAS TUSSER

When the economy takes a nosedive, instead of panicking (the most common reaction), you need to know what you own and how much it's worth. Without this knowledge, it's impossible to make intelligent financial decisions. This chapter will show you how to find all your assets and determine their value. You may be pleasantly surprised!

THE THREE-MINUTE EXPLANATION

If you think that taking a personal inventory of your finances is onerous, think about the difficulties that surrounded one of the world's first inventories—of trees. It took place in eighteenth-century Europe, when wood was prized as the main source of fuel, the way we value oil today. Officials, fearing that the supply would run out, asked hundreds of foresters to estimate the number of trees under their care by eye. Believe me, your audit, aided by a calculator and computer-generated spread-sheets, will be much easier!

Many people do their personal audit and net worth statement at the beginning of each new year—a wise move. But unless you're reading this book in January, don't wait. Do it this weekend.

And resist the temptation to imbibe an "audit ale" to lighten the task. Originally brewed centuries ago at Oxford and Cambridge universities, audit ale was so named because it was drunk to celebrate the completion of the colleges' annual financial accounts. Some historians maintain, however, that audit ale was given to the accountants prior to their scrutinizing the books, in hopes of a more favorable outcome.

If you want to be smart about handling your money, be it a large or small amount, not only should you take a cold, sober look at your financial inventory, but you also should be able to explain what you own and approximately how much it's worth in three minutes or less. The following six steps will enable you to achieve the *three-minute explanation*.

STEP 1: FIND YOUR MONEY

Make a list of all your accounts—at banks, credit unions, mutual fund companies, brokerage firms, or insurance companies. Don't overlook your retirement plans and savings bonds. Include contact name, telephone number, e-mail address, account number, and the value of each as of your last statement.

If this takes you forever, it's possible that you have too many accounts and it's time to consolidate them—not only will you have a better grip on what you have, but you'll also slash the fees and commissions you pay. Here's my basic formula for how many mutual funds you should own:

DOLLAR VALUE OF PORTFOLIO	NUMBER OF FUNDS
$2,000 to $5,000	1 or 2
$5,000 to $20,000	2 to 4
$20,000 to $50,000	4 to 7
$50,000 to $200,000	7 to 10
$200,000 to $600,000	10 to 15
$600,000 and over	15 to 20

Digging Up Savings Bonds

It's easy to forget those savings bonds your grandparents gave you on your birthdays or that you automatically purchased through a payroll savings plan at work. They should be included among your assets on your net worth statement.

Dig into your safe deposit box, your desk drawer, or that trunk in the attic. Once you've assembled them, I recommend using the TreasuryDirect program (www.treasurydirect.gov) to determine their value and to create an up-to-date inventory. If you have the old-fashioned paper E, EE, or I savings bonds, take time to enroll in the new SmartExchange Program, also on this site, or call 800-722-2678. The program converts paper bonds into an electronic account where the funds will be held until maturity.

$ TIP If you can't locate old bonds, download PDF 1048, "Claim for Lost, Stolen or Destroyed United States Savings Bonds."

If you decide not to use TreasuryDirect, then keep clear records of your savings bonds. For each, record the issue date, face amount, and bond number, along with the name, social security number, and address of each person listed on the bond. Then place a copy of your list in your safe deposit box and keep another at home or at your office.

STEP 2: DO A HOUSEHOLD INVENTORY

Fires, floods, and other furies of nature point out the importance of having an up-to-date list of your possessions, accompanied by photos or a video plus estimates of their replacement value (not what you paid for them). Not only is this inventory important for determining how much insurance you need, but the dollar amounts can also be slotted into your net worth statement, as discussed later in this chapter.

Note each item's condition and age. Record serial numbers for electronic equipment, such as computers, fax machines, TVs, DVDs, CD players, cameras, cell phones, and iPods, and also for kitchen appliances and washer-dryers. Back up your visual inventory with as many sales receipts as you can locate.

Keep one copy of your inventory in your safe deposit box and one in your office, and give one to someone who lives out of town. And don't forget to go through your attic, basement, garage, and off-site storage units.

STEP 3: ADD UP YOUR NET WORTH

Finding out how much you're worth may be a pleasant surprise. If it's not, you need to know the truth in order to turn the situation around. If you're not a math whiz or you're still struggling with long division, you're not excused. In fact, determining your net worth is not mathematically difficult. You can use one of the personal software programs, such as Quicken, Mint. com, or Microsoft Money, or simply complete the form in this chapter.

But be sure to tell the truth. There's no advantage to saying that your house is worth $495,000 when it's been evaluated at $310,000. You're only fooling yourself.

To determine your net worth, you simply add up the current value of all your assets (cars, houses, boats, bank and brokerage accounts, life insurance cash value, jewelry, antiques, collectibles, and so on) and subtract your personal liabilities (mortgage, other loans, credit card debt, and so forth).

Regarding your house, you may need to ask your real estate broker to estimate how much it would sell for on the open market. If you have serious jewelry, antiques, paintings, and other such items, you may want to call in an expert appraiser. (This is also well worth doing to make sure that these items are adequately insured.) To find an appraiser in your area, contact

- **American Society of Appraisers,** 800-ASA-VALU, www. appraisers.org
- **Appraiser Association of America,** 212-889-5404, www. appraisersassoc.org

For the book value of your vehicles from the last 21 years, be they coupes, convertibles, or Chevys with fins, consult

- **Kelley Blue Book,** www.kbb.com

This service also evaluates motorcycles, personal watercraft (such as Sea-Doo, Tomoto, Kawasaki, or Jet Skis), ATVs, and even snowmobiles! If you have a camper, trailer, or vintage car, consult the Kelley Blue Book print guides. You may find copies at your public library or, if not, through 800-BLUE-BOOK.

YOUR NET WORTH STATEMENT

ASSETS	CURRENT VALUE
Cash on hand	$
Savings accounts	$
Checking accounts	$
Certificates of deposit	$
Money market accounts	$
Stocks	$
Corporate, municipal, and savings bonds	$
U.S. Treasuries	$
Investment club portfolio	$
Mutual funds	$
Other investments	$
Severance pay	$
Life insurance (cash value)	$
Annuities	$
Retirement funds	
IRA, Keogh, SEP IRA	$
Vested interest in pension or profit-sharing plan	$
401(k) or 403(b)	$
Home (market value minus mortgage)	$
Other real estate (market value)	$
Vehicles (Blue Book value)	$
Sports and hobby equipment	$
Jewelry, furs	$
Collectibles	$
Artwork	$
Antiques	$
Other personal property	$
Equity interest in your business	$
Royalties	$
Miscellaneous	$
Total assets	$

PERSONAL LIABILITIES	AMOUNT
Primary mortgage	$
Home equity loan	$
Second mortgage	$
Credit card balances	$
Vehicle loans	$
Student loans	$
Real estate taxes	$
Miscellaneous debts	$
Total liabilities	**$**
Net Worth =	
assets minus liabilities:	**$**

STEP 4: VISIT YOUR SAFE DEPOSIT BOX

Take a picture or video of its contents. Back this up with a written list of items. This is particularly important if you have old-fashioned stock or bond certificates. It's easy to forget how many shares of each company you actually own.

Another reason for documenting the contents of your safe deposit box is that not all boxes are 100% safe and 100% indestructible. Robberies, although quite rare, occasionally occur. Serious weather and natural disasters have also been known to destroy boxes—a number, you may recall, were hit by Hurricane Katrina.

The items that logically belong in a safe deposit box are those that cannot be replaced or that you will need if your house or apartment is destroyed or seriously damaged. Among these items are

- A copy of your will
- A copy of your living will
- A copy of your power of attorney
- A copy of your burial plot deed
- Stock and bond certificates
- Insurance policies
- Titles to your house and cars
- Your marriage license
- Your divorce decree
- Expensive jewelry
- A videotape of the contents of each room in your house or apartment
- Birth certificates
- Family heirloom documents and pictures

Certain documents that many people think should be in a safe deposit box should not be—the reason being that access to the vault area is limited, usually from 8 or 9 A.M. to 4 or 5 P.M., Monday through Friday. And, of course, banks are not open on national holidays.

In addition, many states, including New York and Florida, seal boxes when the owner dies, so make sure that only copies of your will, living will, and power of attorney, not the originals, are in the box. (The originals should be with your attorney.) Nor should you keep original life insurance policies and deeds to burial plots in your box—these papers are needed right after death.

STEP 5: TAKE YOUR STOCKBROKER OR FINANCIAL ADVISOR TO LUNCH

With a jittery market come huge opportunities to make gains or suffer losses. You want to be at the top of your advisor's call list. While you're at lunch, go over your holdings, selecting stocks to keep and stocks to sell. And set stop loss orders. They protect you on the downside, lock in profits, and are also helpful whenever it's difficult to be in constant touch with your broker, such as when you're on vacation or out of the country.

$ TIP Make sure you pay for the lunch. Not only will your advisor be shocked, but he will definitely remember you and your account.

STEP 6: LOOK FOR UNCLAIMED ASSETS

Government agencies have at least $60 billion and perhaps more in unclaimed assets and missing money. This "lost" money comes in the form of bank and credit union accounts, government benefits, inheritances, life insurance proceeds, mutual funds, pension money, contents of safe deposit boxes, savings bonds, stocks and bonds, paychecks, tax refunds, utility deposits, and the like.

There is no central repository for these monies. Nor is there one database listing all of them. Therefore, if you come upon a company that says it has them all, don't believe it. Before hiring anyone to assist you, set aside some time to do your own research using these resources. Perhaps you'll come into a windfall.

- **NATIONAL ASSOCIATION OF UNCLAIMED PROPERTY ADMINISTRA-TORS (NAUPA),** www.unclaimed.org. Start at this url and connect to the huge national database, www.missing money.com. This enables you to check almost every state's unclaimed funds records in one search. In addition, you can link to the Web sites for the handful of states that don't participate in this particular database.

- **FEDERAL GOVERNMENT.** "The Government May Owe You Money," www.usa.gov/Citizen/Topics/Money_Owed. shtml, has links to U.S. government sites that provide search engines or information about how to track lost tax refunds, bank deposits, and pension benefits. Among them:

  - **TREASURY HUNT** (www.treasurydirect.gov/indiv/tools/ tools_treasuryhunt.htm). You can search here for E bonds that are unclaimed or that have stopped earning interest.

  - **FDIC UNCLAIMED FUNDS** (www.fdic.gov/funds/index. asp). This site will tell you if there are unclaimed funds in your name from a bank that the FDIC has liquidated.

$ TIP You can also search for unclaimed property in the name of a deceased family member, but you'll have to prove that you're the rightful heir or executor of the person's estate to claim the funds.

WordSmarts

ASSETS: Property or investments that can be sold and converted to cash.

LIABILITIES: Debt that you owe and that will follow you should you move.

LIVING WILL: A directive to medical personnel regarding your wishes about medical care at the end of your life if you are unable to communicate.

NET WORTH: The total value of your cash, property, and investments after deducting your liabilities.

POWER OF ATTORNEY: A legal document that grants another person the right to act on your behalf. It may focus on one area (financial or medical, for example) or be all-encompassing. A medical power of attorney, for example, also known as a health-care power of attorney, authorizes someone to make health-care decisions for you if you cannot do so. This person is called your *agent*.

STOP LOSS ORDER: An order in which you direct your broker to buy or sell a stock when it rises or falls to a specified price. It protects profits that have already been made and/or prevents losses if the stock drops further.

FOR FURTHER INFORMATION

FEDERAL CITIZEN INFORMATION CENTER (888-878-3256, www.pueblo.sga.gov) has a wealth of information about managing your assets, including home inventories and tools for creating a savings plan.

INSURANCE INFORMATION INSTITUTE (www.iii.org) has free software programs: "Know Your Stuff," for doing your own home inventory and "Your Financial House" for evaluating your personal financial situation.

2

Protecting Your Money:
Safe Harbors

*"Where large sums of money are concerned,
it is advisable to trust nobody."*
—AGATHA CHRISTIE

Whatever amount you have in a bank or credit union—ideally three to six months' worth of living expenses—safeguarding that money is crucial, especially during a recession. That includes money in an old-fashioned savings account, in a money market deposit account, or in certificates of deposit (CDs). In this chapter, you'll find out just how safe your money is.

When Willie Sutton (1901–1980) was asked by a reporter why he robbed banks, he allegedly said, "Because that's where the money is."

You, too, undoubtedly have money stashed in at least one bank—most likely your local one. Or perhaps you use one down the road from your country house (if you're lucky enough to have a country house), or an Internet bank that's enticed you with its higher-than-usual-yielding CDs. And, hey—maybe you've got an account or two offshore.

Incidentally, the Brooklyn-born Sutton, always impeccably dressed, robbed about 100 banks, stealing nearly $2 million. Frequently imprisoned, he managed to escape several times, once wearing a guard's uniform. On Christmas Eve 1969, he was released from New York State's Attica Prison because of poor health. But that didn't stop him from working—after his parole, he made a TV commercial for the New Britain (CT) Bank & Trust Company, promoting the launch of its photo credit card program!

HOW SAFE IS YOUR BANK ACCOUNT?

On October 3, 2008, President George Bush signed the Emergency Economic Stabilization Act of 2008, which temporarily raised the limit on FDIC bank deposit coverage from $100,000 to $250,000 per depositor.

! CAUTION The coverage for retirement accounts (up to $250,000 per person) was *not* increased.

The increase, however, does include money market deposit accounts. This type of bank demand account pays higher interest than a saving or checking account, and in most banks you're required to maintain a certain minimum balance, typically $2,500 (for a regular money market account) to $100,000 (for a "jumbo" account). You are allowed a limited number of transactions each month—usually three deposits and three withdrawals. You can also write checks against the account.

Obviously, it's prudent to have only up to $250,000 per depositor in one bank, given that that's the cap for FDIC insurance.

That includes brick-and-mortar banks and Internet banks. But there are some nice exceptions you need to know about:

1. In addition to an individual account that is insured up to $250,000, you can also have a joint account, in which up to $500,000 is insured ($250,000 for each person). Your joint account can be with a spouse, a child, or anyone else.

2. In addition to $250,000 in an individual account and $500,000 in a joint account, retirement account deposits are insured up to $250,000 per plan depositor. These include IRAs, SEP IRAs, and Keoghs.

3. Accounts that are registered in a living trust are insured up to $250,000 per owner, per beneficiary.

Based on the 2008 increased FDIC coverage, here's how you could insure up to $1.5 million in one bank. The dollar amounts for each type of account given here are the maximum that can be insured.

ACCOUNT OWNER	ACCOUNT BALANCE
Dick's savings account and CDs	$250,000
Jane's savings account and CDs	$250,000
Dick and Jane's joint savings account	$500,000
Dick, trustee for Jane	$250,000
Jane, trustee for Dick	$250,000
TOTAL DEPOSITS INSURED:	**$1,500,000**

$ TIP To make certain that all your money in an old-fashioned or Internet bank is insured and that you're not over the limit, check with MS EDIE, the Electronic Deposit Insurance Estimator. You'll find EDIE at www.fdic.gov. Click on "Consumer Resources." If you don't have Internet access, call 877-275-3342 to reach a live person.

MS EDIE, the Electronic Deposit Insurance Estimator, spells out how much of your money at a bank is insured and how much, if any, has exceeded the limits. *If EDIE tells you that some of your money is not insured, you have two choices.*

First, you could move the uninsured amount to another FDIC-insured institution on your own. To find savings accounts and CDs with the highest interest rates in the country, check with Bankrate, Inc., www.bankrate.com.

Second, you could use a bank that participates in the CDARS Program. That stands for Certificate of Deposit Account Registry Service, a network of some 2,500 banks throughout the United States.

When you deposit more than $100,000 with a bank that is in the CDARS system, that bank will place your money in CDs with other banks around the nation. Thus, you gain both the convenience of managing all your CDs through one institution and the peace of mind that comes from knowing that 100% of your deposits are FDIC covered.

To find a bank near you that participates in CDARS, go to www.cdars.com.

WHAT IS THE FDIC?

The Federal Deposit Insurance Corporation is an independent federal government agency. It was founded in 1933 because so many banks had failed during the late 1920s and early 1930s.

The FDIC insures deposits (savings accounts, money market funds, IRAs, and certificates of deposit) in member banks and thrift institutions. It has two sources of funding: premiums paid by member banks and thrifts, and earnings it receives from its investments in U.S. Treasuries. It does *not* receive money from Congress.

! CAUTION The FDIC does not insure securities or mutual funds offered to the public by banks.

As we go to press, banks pay an average assessment of 12 to 14 basis points to the FDIC in order to cover their deposits. A basis point is the equivalent of 1 cent for every $100 in a savings account.

$ TIP While the vast majority of banks have FDIC coverage, you can make certain by going to Bank Find at www.fdic.gov and then clicking on "Deposit Insurance."

WHEN A BANK FAILS

In 2008, some 25 banks failed. Although it's not likely, it could happen to your bank. If it does, go to the FDIC's "Failed Banks List" at www.fdic.gov/bank/individual/failed/banklist.html. On the right, under "Consumer Resources," click on "Failed Banks" and then on the name of your bank to find out what institution took it over and to get information about your old bank's ATMs, safe deposit boxes, wire services, processed checks, loans, and interest paid on savings accounts and CDs. (You'll also find a telephone number to call for additional help.)

$ TIP If you don't have Internet access, you can call the FDIC at 1-877-ASK-FDIC (275-3342).

If you're worried about a possible bank failure, you may find the official takeover procedure reassuring. It's smooth and well organized.

When a bank can't meet its obligations, the FDIC moves in temporarily and runs the bank for a short time while auctioning off its assets to another bank. The change in ownership usually takes place over a weekend. For example, in 2008, when the FDIC arranged for SunTrust Bank in Florida to assume the insured deposits of the failed First Priority Bank, all branches of First Priority closed on Friday and opened Monday morning as SunTrust branches.

All insured First Priority depositors automatically became insured SunTrust depositors. However, the failed bank had about 840 accounts that exceeded the federal insurance cap. The people holding those accounts had to wait to gain access to their money. Why the wait? Because the uninsured accounts were credited over time as the FDIC sold them to healthy banks.

Note: If the FDIC cannot find a bank to buy an insolvent institution's assets, it mails checks to those account holders who are within the federal insurance limits. Interest is paid right up until the night the bank is closed.

THE FDIC'S BANK WATCH LIST

The FDIC maintains a list of troubled or potentially troubled banks. However, as it acknowledges, it never reveals the list to the public.

Nonetheless, you can get bank ratings from a number of companies. Veribanc (www.veribanc.com, 800-442-2657) charges $10 for the first "short" report via telephone, $5 per short telephone report thereafter, and $25 to $110 for longer written reports. Bauer Financial (www.bauerfinancial.com, 800-388-6686) provides a first "highlights" report for $10 and additional ones for $4 each, as well as longer reports for $20 to $99. Bauer Financial also rates banks and credit unions (on a scale of 1 to 5) on its Web site.

$ TIP You can get a free report (with a 1 to 5 rating) from Bankrate, Inc. Its "Safe & Sound Service" (www.bankrate.com/brm/safe sound/ss_home.asp) evaluates the financial strength of thousands of banks, thrifts, and credit unions, rating each on a scale of 1 to 5. Search by name of the institution, state, zip code, asset size, or rating.

THE BENEFITS OF LADDERING

One of the easiest ways to make certain that you have money available (for spending or reinvesting) is to ladder bank CDs. This investment strategy involves buying bank certificates of deposit with different maturity dates.

For example, you could buy one CD that comes due in 6 months, one that comes due in 9 months, one in 12 months, and one in 24 months. As each matures and you receive your money, you can buy a new CD or use your check to pay college tuition bills, reduce your mortgage, or meet other financial goals. If you're out of work, laddering (which can also be done with bonds and U.S. Treasuries) provides a regular stream of cash.

A laddered portfolio also gives you protection against changes in interest rates—if rates go up, you've got money coming due that can be used to purchase a new, higher-yielding CD. If rates go down, you can invest the money in high-dividend-paying stocks, a mutual fund, or an annuity.

$ TIP For the nation's highest-yielding bank CDs, along with information about minimum dollar amounts, check with Bankrate, Inc., www.bankrate.com.

HOW SAFE ARE MONEY MARKET FUNDS?

Money market funds, which are offered by almost all mutual fund companies, have traditionally not been federally insured. Nevertheless, they have been considered safe because they are liquid, solid, and conservative—liquid in that you can take out your money at any time, solid in that they maintain a per share value of $1, and conservative in that they invest in debt issued by highly rated companies and government entities.

They also tend to pay higher interest rates than bank savings accounts or Treasuries, adding to their appeal.

So it's not surprising that both individual investors, like you and me, and institutions have used money market funds for years as places to park money while waiting to invest it elsewhere or simply as a place for one's nest egg.

Nevertheless, money market funds have not been as safe as FDIC-insured bank accounts, no matter what you read elsewhere. For example, in 1994, Community Bank's U.S. Government Fund saw its shares fall below $1 in the wake of the Orange County (California) bankruptcy. Investors got back 94 cents on the dollar.

Then in September 2008, the Reserve Primary Money Market Fund "broke the buck," with investors getting back 97 cents on the dollar. This $64 billion fund collapsed because it had invested heavily in Lehman Brothers debt, which, of course, as you know, became worthless when Lehman Brothers filed for bankruptcy.

Agatha Christie was right on target when she said you should trust nobody with large sums of your money.

THE BOTTOM LINE: Money market mutual funds have not been FDIC insured—until recently.

In September 2008, the U.S. Treasury Department announced that it was establishing a temporary "guarantee program" for money market mutual funds, through which the mutual fund companies could buy federal insurance. The Treasury is guaranteeing the share price of any participating money market fund whose shares fall below $1.

$ TIP   If you have a money market mutual fund, call the toll-free customer service number immediately and ask if the fund is participating in the government's guarantee program. If the answer is no, put your money in a fund that is, ideally one that is offered by a large, solvent company such as Fidelity, T. Rowe Price, Vanguard, or Schwab. Theoretically these companies are large enough to deal with a run on their funds.

And, make certain that the fund is regulated as a 2a-7 fund, publicly offered and registered with the SEC. These funds follow provisions put in place by the Treasury to maintain the $1 per share value.

SIX SAFE HAVENS FOR $600

No place except under your mattress is totally safe—and even then your kids might find your stash. These six picks, however, are as safe as you can get in the outside world.

1. SAVINGS ACCOUNTS. These are FDIC-insured up to $250,000 per depositor. Among the highest yielding in this category is that offered by INGdirect, which has a current rate of 2.20% for its Orange Savings Account. The minimum is $1, and the account is electronically linked to your current checking account. Transfers are free. For details, go to www.ingdirect.com.

2. REWARDCHECKING ACCOUNTS. Insured by the FDIC, National Credit Union Administration (NCUA), or American Share Insurance (ASI), these are offered by smaller banks, have no minimum requirements, and offer refunds for fees if you use another bank's ATM; some of these accounts are currently yielding as much as 5.5%. You are required to use the bank's debit card several times a month. For details, go to www.checkingfinder.com.

3. SERIES I SAVINGS BONDS. Backed by the U.S. government, these give you a hedge against future inflation. The interest rate is a combination of a fixed rate plus an inflation rate that is adjusted twice a year; it is 5.64% through April 30, 2009. If you redeem I bonds within the first five years, you'll forfeit the three most recent months' interest. After five years, you won't be penalized. For details, go to www.savingsbonds.gov.

4. BANK CDS. These FDIC-insured certificates have higher yields the further out their maturity is. Flagstar Bank is paying 3.25% on a one-year $500 CD and 3.9% on a five-year $500 CD. For details, call 800-642-0039, or go to www.flagstar.com.

$ TIP Search for the highest rates at www.bankrate.com.

5. UTILITY STOCKS. Well-run utility companies offer a product that everyone needs. Select a company rated 1 for safety and 1 for timeliness by the Value Line Investment Survey. You can purchase $600 worth of almost any stock at BuyandHold.com.

6. DIVIDEND-PAYING STOCKS. Companies that continually pay dividends are financially sound enough to do so. Check Standard & Poor's "S&P 500 Dividend Aristocrats." This list of 52 companies that have increased their dividends every year for 25 consecutive years makes a good base for long-term investors, especially those who reinvest their dividends. The Aristocrats currently range from GE, with an 11.40% yield, to Sigma-Aldrich and Questar, both yielding 1.40%. Before adding an Aristocrat to your portfolio, check its rating with the Value Line Investment Survey. For details, go to www.marketattributes.stand ardandpoors.com. In the middle of the table, click on "Dividend Aristocrats."

(See Chapter 8 for advice on how to use the Value Line Investment Survey, an independently published weekly that covers more than 1,700 stocks.)

THE CREDIT UNION ADVANTAGE

Edward Filene, a Boston merchant and founder of Filene's bargain basement, was instrumental in the passage of the first state credit union act. The year was 1909. While credit unions were initially designed to help working-class people who did not qualify for commercial bank loans, today there are 8,600 federally insured credit unions in the United States and close to 600 that are provincially governed in Canada. If you can join one, be smart and do so. The benefits are excellent.

Because they are not-for-profit associations, owned by their members and operated mainly by volunteer boards, they have low overhead costs. That, in turn, means that they can offer savers higher rates and borrowers lower rates than regular banks.

Most credit unions have automatic payroll deduction plans, savings and checking accounts, mortgages and home equity loans, car loans, credit cards, IRAs, and other accounts similar to money market accounts and CDs.

Credit unions are actually not-for-profit cooperatives in which people pool their savings and then lend money and provide other services to one another. Federal law requires that the members of a credit union must have a common bond, such as working for the same employer or government agency or belonging to the same club, church, synagogue, or other group.

The "common bond" guidelines were broadened a few years ago to include a specific community or neighborhood. Still, about 80% of credit unions have an occupational or associational bond.

Though the specifics vary by credit union, family members (spouse, partner, parents, grandparents, children, siblings, aunts, and uncles) of an eligible member are usually permitted to join as well.

Among the larger, better-known credit unions are Navy Federal Credit Union (in Virginia), Golden 1 Credit Union (in California), and Boeing Employees Credit Union (in Washington).

> **$ TIP** If you would like to become a member of a credit union, contact the Credit Union National Association (CUNA) at: 800-356-9655, www.creditunion.coop. Its Web site also has a chart comparing credit union and commercial savings and loan rates, with credit unions coming out on top.

Make certain that the credit union you belong to is insured by the National Credit Union Administration (800-755-1030, www.ncua.gov), a federal agency. The NCUA insures 80 million account holders for up to $250,000, with guidelines similar to those used by the FDIC.

THE ADVANTAGES OF SMALLER BANKS

In an effort to attract customers, more than 560 smaller community banks and credit unions now offer high-yield checking accounts with full liquidity and high interest rates. Rates, in fact, are well above those paid on CDs and money market accounts by these banks' larger competitors. These accounts, part of a program called REWARDChecking developed by BancVue of Texas, are insured by the FDIC or, in the case of credit unions, by the NCUA or ASI.

REWARDChecking accounts have neither minimum deposit requirements nor monthly fees. However, to earn these higher rates (topping out at 5.5% as we go to press), you'll need to use your account's debit card a specified number of times a month (typically 12 to 15) and to get your monthly statement by e-mail.

Because these smaller banks may not have a convenient ATM machine near you, they rebate ATM fees each month up to a specified amount.

To find a bank or credit union nearby that offers the RE-WARDChecking account, go to www.checkingfinder.com. Here you'll also learn what rates are across the nation and how much you can earn each year based on your average balance.

WordSmarts

ANNUITY: A contract, usually sold by an insurance company, that makes periodic payments to the person who holds it. Payments can begin immediately or be deferred, often until the annuitant's retirement begins. Annuities can have either a fixed or a variable interest rate.

BASIS POINT: A value equal to 1/100 of 1%.

BREAK THE BUCK: When a money market mutual fund's value falls below $1 per share.

LADDERING: An investment strategy in which CDs or bonds with differing maturities are assembled in a portfolio. Because of the varying maturity dates, the owner has a regular stream of cash coming in that can then be reinvested.

LIVING TRUST: A bank deposit account, owned by one or more people, indicating that the money in the account will go to a named beneficiary or beneficiaries upon the death of the owner(s). Trusts can be revocable or irrevocable. For information, go to www.fdic.gov. Click on "Your Insured Deposits" and then on "Ownership Categories."

MUTUAL FUND: An investment vehicle in which investors' dollars are pooled with those of thousands of others. The combined total is invested by a professional manager in a variety of securities (cash, stocks, bonds, or government paper). Mutual fund shares are sold to the public.

SEC: The Securities and Exchange Commission, a federal agency created in 1934 to administer U.S. securities laws. It consists of five members, appointed by the president for five-year staggered terms. Among its responsibilities are registration of securities listed on stock exchanges, disclosure of insider holdings, and regulation of stockbrokers and dealers. For information, go to www. sec.gov.

FOR FURTHER INFORMATION

GET IT TOGETHER: ORGANIZE YOUR RECORDS, 3d ed., by Melanie Cullen (Berkeley, Calif.: Nolo Press, 2008).

TEACH YOURSELF THRIFTY LIVING, by Barty Phillips (New York, N.Y.: McGraw-Hill, 2008).

3

Buttoning Down:
The Frugal Budget

"Money is a terrible master but an excellent servant."

—P. T. BARNUM

A recession may serve to remind us that we don't have unlimited supplies of cash, but smart people mind their pennies in all economic cycles. You can be one of them!

You need not be as parsimonious as Henry David Thoreau was between 1845 and 1847. But you might think about how happy the writer/philosopher was living in the one-room, 10" × 15" shingled cabin that he built—with a borrowed ax—at Walden Pond. It was here that he wrote essays, entertained friends, caught fish, and communed with nature. He also planted acres of produce that he ate and sold, earning $23.44 in his first year as a farmer. He turned the journal of his experience into the American classic *Walden; or Life in the Woods*. As he wrote:

For two years and two months, all my expenses have amounted to but 27 cents a week, and I have fared gloriously in all respects.

Thoreau obviously wasn't trying to keep up with the Joneses, and neither should you—there will always be at least one Jones with more money than you.

THE ABBREVIATED BUDGET

You've undoubtedly read that you should keep a detailed budget, noting your income and expenses. That's a fine idea, and if you have the *patience* and *fortitude** to do so, I applaud you. But I'm not going to take up precious space here explaining how to do it—you're reading this, so you're smart, and Quicken and Microsoft Money both have fill-in budget spreadsheets that are easy to use.

Instead, I urge you to undertake my *abbreviated budget*. It involves buying an old-fashioned notebook and writing down everything you spend for one month. This alone will provide a clear wake-up call regarding how you're handling money.

IF YOU CAN'T PAY YOUR BILLS

Begin by calling a family conference. Your spouse, partner, roommate, and older children should be invited to participate.

---

*   Patience and Fortitude are the names of the two lion statues outside the huge (and wonderful) New York City Public Library on Fifth Avenue at 42nd Street. No one is quite sure, however, who is who or which is which. I mention them because your own public library can play a key role in your budget, as you'll see later.

Conquering the situation will require cooperation from all older members of your family.

Then line up your bills on your kitchen table or computer screen and prioritize them. Place the basic "must pay" items at the top of the list: groceries, utilities, transportation, your mortgage, and health insurance premiums. Next, if you've lost your job, list the expenses involved in looking for new employment: your Internet and cell phone services, résumé preparation, and travel.

(For specific suggestions about handling your mortgage, see Chapter 6, and for handling credit card debt, see Chapter 7.)

Now, make a list of things you don't need, the nonnecessities in your life. These are officially called *variable expenses*. You might be able to scale back on premium cable TV, operating two cars, vacations, fresh flowers, box seats at the game, or playing the slots. For more suggestions, see the list on page 30.) If this lineup seems arduous, remember that it's temporary— only until you get back on your feet.

Finally, discuss with your family ways in which you can join together and reduce common expenses, such as carpooling (to work and to your children's schools and activities), taking public transportation (forget taxis if you live in a city; hop on the bus or subway), and buying thermoses for everyone (skip vending machines and coffee to go). If you or your kids have friends over for dinner, instead of providing the entire meal, turn it into a potluck affair.

Share membership dues at your gym or Y with a friend. Plan to read magazines and check out books, CDs, and videos at your public library. Most now have free Internet access plus public computers.

If you regularly shop for clothes at department stores, switch to discount outlets and secondhand shops. Make only pre-planned shopping trips, and shop with a list. If shopping with a friend encourages you to buy more, go solo. Or take along a thrifty friend who will tell you why you don't need yet another pair of black shoes.

Before you buy a navy blue sweater, go through your drawers. Most of us have more than enough items in our closets and bureaus to last a lifetime. Chances are, you already have a navy blue sweater—maybe two! And if your closets are overstuffed, "simplify, simplify," as Thoreau said, and get cash by taking your excess to a consignment shop for resale.

AN A TO Z OF VARIABLE EXPENSES

If your spending is outpacing your income, review this list and check off at least four items that you can cut back on or eliminate entirely.

☐ Books	☐ Gifts
☐ Cable TV	☐ Groceries
☐ Cell phone use	☐ Hair salon
☐ Clothing	☐ Home improvements
☐ Club dues and charges	☐ Housekeeper
☐ Collecting (art, antiques, coins, etc.)	☐ Landscaping, yard maintenance, snow shoveling
☐ Cosmetics	☐ Liquor
☐ Drugstore purchases	☐ Magazine subscriptions
☐ Dry cleaning	☐ Restaurant dining
☐ Entertainment	☐ Transportation
☐ Flowers	☐ Vacations

CONSERVE YOUR CASH

In addition to shopping less, spending less, and eating home more, you can conserve cash by changing how you pay for certain items. This is of the utmost importance if you are out of work or fear you will be.

Begin by putting an end to automatic withdrawals from your checking and/or savings accounts. You now want to control every penny that you spend and, equally important, when it's spent. If you no longer have a regular paycheck and you're living on unemployment or severance, you may find it necessary to change the dates when you pay your bills. You can't do this if the payments are on automatic pilot. And if you run out of money, an automatic payment will trigger an overdraft fee, adding further to your cash flow problems.

In terms of when bills are paid, pay your mortgage, utilities, groceries, medications, and health insurance first.

You can also conserve cash by making only minimum payments. If, for example, you've been making extra payments on your mortgage, start paying just the minimum required by your lender.

And, if absolutely necessary, make only minimum payments on your credit cards. I say *absolutely* because interest on unpaid balances is high and mounts up quickly.

THE BOTTOM LINE: Resist the temptation to use credit cards to hang on to your old lifestyle, the lifestyle you had when you were working. Use cards only when emergencies arise, such as job-hunting expenses, car repairs, and medications that are not covered by insurance.

CONTACT YOUR CREDITORS

Another step you can take if you've run out of cash or are seriously struggling is to call your creditors. You may be surprised at how many of them are willing to negotiate a new payment schedule.

Place these calls right away. You want to be the one making the first move. In other words, don't wait until you start receiving dunning calls or letters from bill collectors. Explain your situation. Ask for a grace period, and indicate how much money you can send each month.

If the person you speak with stonewalls you or if you're told that nothing can be done, ask to be transferred to that employee's supervisor.

Be sure to take notes. Write down the date and time of the call and the first and last names of people you speak with. Then jot down the terms of agreement. Send a typed letter (in addition to an e-mail) confirming the new agreement. Keep a copy for your files.

NINE WAYS TO CUT EVERYDAY EXPENSES

In addition to the previous suggestions:

1. DON'T SMOKE. In addition to jeopardizing your health, smoking is expensive. A pack of cigarettes costs $3 in Florida, $5 in Texas, $6.50 in Massachusetts, and $9 in my hometown, New York City. If you smoke two packs a day, that adds up to as much as $18 a day. You do the math for a year.

$ TIP Plus, nonsmokers get lower rates on health and automobile insurance.

2. DINE AT HOME. Restaurants are one of the biggest nonessential items in the American budget. If you don't have time to cook or you always burn the toast, pick up food at your local Chinese or other inexpensive restaurant and take it home. You'll save at least 15% because you won't have to tip the waiter or pay for soft drinks, wine, or beer. And you'll probably have leftovers for yet another meal.

3. BUT DON'T GO COLD TURKEY. Dining out now and then is fun for everyone. When you do, skip the starter, stick with the house wine, and have coffee and dessert at home. You can also save by taking advantage of any early bird specials and coupons (in your mailbox and newspaper circulars). Note: Some restaurants allow diners to share huge entrees for free or for a small charge.

$ TIP Discount dining programs will help you cut costs. Check out the following programs:

- Rewards Network (877-491-3436, www.rewardsnetwork. com) rebates your credit card (AMEX, Visa, or others) for up to 15% of the cost of meals, beverages, tax, and tip at thousands of restaurants in the United States and Canada. It will send you lists of places to eat in your neighborhood. Membership: free.
- Primecard (800-444-8872, www.igtcard.com), a restaurant charge card, gives you up to 50% off meals and purchases at 1,000 restaurants and entertainment and retail establishments in New York, New Jersey, Connecticut, and South Florida. Membership: $25 per year.

4. PUMP YOUR OWN GAS. Depending on where you live, you can save 10 cents per gallon if you open the car door, get out, and do it yourself.

5. BROWN-BAG IT. If you spend $8 a day on a sandwich, coffee or soda, and a candy bar (and that's being modest), that adds up to $2,000 a year, assuming two weeks off for vacation. Boost that to $10 a day and we're talking at least $2,500 a year.

6. BIKE IT. We mentioned carpooling and taking public transportation earlier. But keep in mind that the cheapest, healthiest, and greenest ways to get from point A to point B are walking and biking. And, you'll also be giving up the stress of traffic jams and gridlock.

$ TIP The American Recovery and Reinvestment Act, known as the stimulus package, signed by President Obama in February 2009, gives a tax break for people who take public transit to work and whose employer subsidizes their parking or transit costs. Employees can now set aside up to $230 a month (in pretax dollars) to cover the cost of a van pool, bus, or train. That's up from $120. Employees can also set aside up to $230 a month for parking. If your company is not reimbursing parking and/or transit costs, get together with your colleagues and ask management to get on the band wagon.

7. TALK SMARTER. Make sure you have the cheapest telephone calling plan. Keep checking. Verizon, for example, continually comes up with new money-savers, hoping to keep its customers—though you have to ask for them.

Most important, make sure you have the service that meets your local and long distance calling patterns. That might be unlimited calling or the cheapest per minute rate. Go over past bills to discover your patterns.

$ TIP Two Web sites that find the lowest per minute rate are www.saveonphone.com and www.phonedog.com.

A prepaid or pay-as-you-go cell phone plan could be less expensive than a pricey cell contract—if you are willing to limit your cell phone usage. Check the pros and cons of leading plans at www.prepaidreviews.com.

7. TOSS THE CATALOGS. When they arrive in your mailbox, don't even peek inside; doing so opens pages and pages of temptation.

$ TIP Get off mailing lists by contacting the Direct Mail Association's Mail Preference Service: 212-768-7277, www.DMAChoice.org.

8. RUN AN ENERGY CHECK. Call your utility company and ask if it has time-of-day pricing. If so, you'll be guaranteed lower rates if you don't use your appliances during peak periods—for example, if you do your laundry after 8 P.M., when power usage is at its lowest.

$ TIP Be sure to talk to your utility company about how to monitor your electricity for two weeks to make sure that time-of-day pricing will indeed save you money.

And ask your company to give you a free energy checkup. Most will come to your house, do an inspection, and recommend specific ways to reduce your bill. You could save 7% to 25% per month.

$ TIP "Energy Savers," available from the U.S. Department of Energy (877-337-3463, www.energysavers.gov), is full of useful tips.

The 2009 stimulus package increased the tax break for homeowners who make energy-saving improvements. The energy-efficient home improvement credit was increased from $500 to $1,500 per home.

You may be entitled to a break on your state taxes as well. A number of states are now giving residents tax credits for energy-efficient home improvements. To find out if your state is one of them, check with the Database of State Incentives for Renewable Energy at www.dsireusa.org.

9. FIND A DISCOUNT CODE BEFORE SHOPPING. A growing number of online retailers offer discount codes—not all the time, but certainly some of the time. And several Web sites track these codes and provide details about them. So before you purchase an item online, browse these free sites. You may get a discount or free shipping—or both—just for doing a little research.

www.bradsdeals.com
www.couponcabin.com
www.currentcodes.com
www.retailmenot.com
www.thedailygreen

HELP PAYING FOR HEAT

If you're struggling to pay your bills, you may be among the thousands of people who are entitled for help from the Low Income Home Energy Assistance Program (LIHEAP), run by the Administration for Children and Families (part of the U.S. Department of Health and Human Services). You may be eligible if you or someone in your home is elderly, disabled, or under six years old. In addition to help with paying your heating costs, LIHEAP provides assistance with weatherizing homes and making energy-related home repairs.

For information on how to apply, visit www.acf.hhs.gov/programs/ocs/liheap or call the National Assistance Referral (NEAR) project at 866-674-6327.

HOW TO CUT YOUR
GROCERY STORE COSTS

The cost of milk, bread, eggs, cheese, and just about everything else has gone up this year. Yet you, your family, Fido, and Kitty must eat. Here are 22 ways to buy what you need while spending less.

Before Leaving Home

1. MAKE A LIST. This is so obvious, yet many shoppers run out the door without a list in hand. Writing down what you really need helps you reduce expensive impulse purchases. Then check your list against your inventory. You may have forgotten that your pantry holds enough canned vegetables to get you through the entire winter.

2. MAKE A SEPARATE LIST FOR TOILETRIES AND PAPER PRODUCTS. They're less pricey at Walgreens, RiteAid, Costco, Sam's Club, BJ's, and the like.

3. CLIP COUPONS. But do so selectively. Use coupons only for items that are on your list or for items that you know will be on next week's list.

4. HAVE A MEAL OR AT LEAST A SNACK. It's a no-brainer, but one we're likely to forget. If you're hungry, you'll automatically buy more than you need, and you'll wind up adding items to your cart that you can eat immediately, before getting home. So never shop on an empty stomach.

5. ARRANGE YOUR FAMILY'S TIME SO THAT YOU CAN SHOP ALONE. Or at least, shop without the children in tow. Kids are great at talking their parents into buying something that's unnecessarily expensive. You may also find that you purchase more if you shop with a friend. Your spouse or partner, on the other hand, may have a leveling effect on spending.

6. PLAN TO SHOP ON DOUBLE COUPON DAYS. This applies, of course, only if you use coupons.

7. PUT A CALCULATOR IN YOUR PURSE OR YOUR POCKET. Use it to keep a running tally of the items in your cart. It will also come in handy for comparing unit prices. Generally speaking, bigger is cheaper, but not always.

On the Way to the Store

8. GET CASH. Using debit and credit cards automatically makes it easier to spend more. Put the amount you've budgeted for groceries in an envelope or a special section of your wallet.

At the Store

9. PICK THE RIGHT STORE. Convenience store prices are usually outrageous. Check out food warehouses as well as supermarkets.

10. STUDY THE STORE'S LAYOUT. Typically milk (the number one item purchased in America), ice cream, and other dairy products and also meat are at the rear of the store. This is intentional because it means that you must walk by a lot of other items before you get to your destination.

11. RETURN YOUR CANS AND BOTTLES. It's a pain, but you will get your deposit back.

12. RESIST BOTTLED WATER. It doesn't matter if it's from Italy, France, or Maine. Most cities and towns have decent tap water. If for some reason you don't care for your local water, buy a filter.

13. THINK STORE LABEL. Brand-name items typically cost more. According to a taste test done by Consumer Reports, store brands are often just as good as or better than name brands.

14. STUDY END-OF-THE-AISLE DEALS CAREFULLY. These items may simply be features and not lower-priced items. Many stores promote seasonal items in these prime spaces, such as candy for Halloween and bread stuffing and canned pumpkin for Thanksgiving.

And manufacturers often pay extra for these great locations.

15. GO FOR SOFT DRINKS IN LARGE BOTTLES. It's much cheaper. Then buy a funnel so that you can refill smaller, easier-to-handle bottles at home.

16. AVOID SINGLE SERVINGS. You'll pay dearly for the convenience.

17. SKIP THE P'S. That means prepared, precut, and peeled. Those cubes of watermelon, cantaloupe, pineapple, and strawberries mixed into a plastic container are priced to include the cost of labor. Do your own slicing and dicing. Prepared sandwiches, wraps, and school lunch-box items also add up quickly.

18. SKIP THE G'S. Grated items, that is. Grate your own carrots, cheese, and potatoes.

19. BEND YOUR KNEES. Higher-priced items tend to be at eye level. Lower-priced groceries are often on the bottom shelf.

20. WATCH THE BILL. If you've been keeping a running tally on your calculator, hit "total" before you reach checkout. Then make sure your amounts match those on the scanner.

21. LOOK THE OTHER WAY AT CHECKOUT. Do you really need those magazines, recipe booklets, candy bars, and gadgets?

Finally

22. GROCERY GAME. If you buy a lot of groceries every week, it may be worth the $10 fee (good for eight weeks) to register with the Grocery Game (www.GroceryGame.com).

The site provides a list of products that will be on sale at your favorite supermarket. The list is available before the standard circulars are sent in the mail or are actually available in the stores. The store's individual coupons are also posted.

Another helpful source is Cool Savings (www.coolsavings. com).

SIMPLE MOVES TO SAVE DOLLARS AND ENERGY

1. Do your laundry and run the dishwasher at off-peak hours: nights, early mornings, and weekends.

2. Always run a full load.

3. Clean or replace air conditioner filters once a month.

4. Use fans to circulate air.

5. Keep refrigerator coils clean.

6. Replace incandescent bulbs with compact fluorescent bulbs (CFLs). According to the Alliance to Save Energy (202-857-0666, www.ase.org), if every household in the country replaced just one bulb, we would save as much energy as is consumed by 1 million cars in one year.

7. Buy energy-efficient appliances. Check with Energy Star (888-782-7937, www.energystar.gov) for a list of retailers selling energy-efficient appliances, lighting fixtures, ACs, home office equipment, windows, and electronics. You can also search by product. And type in your zip code to find out if there are special rebates being offered in your city or town.

HOW TO CUT YOUR INSURANCE PREMIUMS

If you have both automobile and homeowners insurance, you can cut costs if you

1. USE THE SAME INSURANCE COMPANY. You can further boost your savings if you carry other lines of coverage, such as an umbrella policy or business insurance. Savings: Up to 15%.

2. ARE LOYAL. Some companies offer additional discounts for policies held for three or more years. Savings: 5 to 10%.

3. COMPARISON SHOP. Loyalty discounts are nice, but you might do better elsewhere. At least a month before your policies renew, call several local agents for quotes and then go to Progressive Insurance (800-PROGRESSIVE, www.progressive. com), Insure (800-324-6370, www.insure.com), and InsWeb (www.insweb.com).

4. PAY PREMIUMS ANNUALLY OR THROUGH AN AUTOMATIC DEBIT FROM YOUR CHECKING ACCOUNT. Otherwise, you'll pay more because of the interest or service fees that are added on. Savings: $2 to $7 a month.

Regarding Car Insurance

5. INCREASE YOUR DEDUCTIBLE. Decide that you'll pay for small accidents out of pocket and raise your deductible, say from $250 to $1,000. The point of insurance is to protect you from major, not minor, accidents. Savings: As much as 15%, sometimes more.

6. SKIP COLLISION COVERAGE. If you're driving an old clunker, you can drop the collision coverage. Insurers will not pay out more than a vehicle's book value, even if it's totally ruined in an accident. Never pay more in collision coverage than your car is worth. Savings: Up to 25%.

7. BE A GROUPIE. You may be able to insure your car, real estate, and life through your employer. Check with your benefits manager. If not, make a list of all the groups, professional associations, and organizations of which you're a member. Include your college. One or more of them is likely to sponsor a discount plan. Savings: 5% or more.

And, if you are or were in the armed forces, contact USAA (800-531-8722, www.usaa.com). The company maintains that its policyholders save up to $600 a year.

8. TAKE ADVANTAGE OF BEING RETIRED, OR EVEN FIRED. If you're no longer commuting to work or if you've started to work from home, negotiate for a lower premium. Savings: 5% or more.

9. BUY A USED CAR. It will cost significantly less to insure. Savings: Up to 30% in some cases.

!CAUTION: Cars that were declared lemons and then repurchased by car manufacturers are often resold on used car lots. Before buying a used model, check its Vehicle Identification Number (VIN) at www.autocheck.com or www.carfax. com. Both sites allow you to review the car's history. Fees start at $15 per car.

And have your mechanic look at any used car you're considering. If you don't have a mechanic, head for an inspection center that is certified by the Car Care Council (www.carcare. org). This organization educates motorists on car maintenance and safety.

10. SPEAK UP FOR ADDITIONAL DISCOUNTS. You're entitled to them, but they are rarely advertised. Tell the insurance company about any of the following that apply. The driver . . .

- Passed driver ed*
- Has other insurance with the company
- Is accident-free
- Is a student with good grades
- Is a college student living on campus without a car
- Is in a car pool
- Is a member of AARP
- Is over age 50
- Is insuring more than one car
- Is a member of a preferred profession (engineer, scientist, or teacher, to name a few)

11. SLOW DOWN. A clean driving record can qualify you for a "good driver" discount. This means that you can't have more than one minor blemish, such as a speeding ticket or noninjury accident, on your driving record in a three-year period. Savings: Up to 20%.

12. DRIVE A LOW-PROFILE CAR. Hot models, all sports cars, and luxury numbers cost much more to insure than the more pedestrian models, principally because they have higher theft rates. For a list of the most frequently stolen cars, check with the Insurance Information Institute at www.iii.org.

13. GET THE RIGHT DEVICES. Certain ones reduce costs, including

- A hood-locking device

---

* Check with AARP (800-350-7025, www.aarp.org/drive) about its driver safety program for people of all ages, members and nonmembers.

- Airbags

- A wheel-locking device

- A security alarm

- An ignition cutoff system

14. GIVE YOURSELF CREDIT. Your credit score can play a role in setting your auto insurance premium in many states. If you're a good credit risk, insurance companies figure you're a better insurance risk, too.

If you've had some problems with your FICO credit score but have recently managed to raise it, tell your insurer. If the company uses an insurance risk score and reruns your numbers, you could now fall into a better risk pool, which will mean a lower premium. A recent study shows that more than 50% of drivers and homeowners pay less in premiums as a result of favorable credit scores.

Also, if you have some unpaid parking tickets (or even unpaid library bills), your city may have passed your unpaid account on to a debt-collection agency. If that agency then ends up reporting the unpaid bill to the credit bureaus, your FICO credit score could take a hit, which can affect your insurance risk score.

15. MAKE THE GRADE. Your child's academic record will come into play when you add him to your insurance policy. Good grades translate into lower premiums. Savings: If your child is a full-time student in high school or college and maintains at least a 3.0 GPA, the cost of adding him to your policy could be cut by as much as 25%.

THE "DRIVE LESS, PAY LESS" PROGRAM

Officially called Pay-As-You-Drive insurance, PAYD is based on the assumption that the less you drive, the less likely it is that you will have an accident. There are two major players in the field; check also with your insurer.

THE MYRATE PLAN (for cars made after 1996) is offered by Progressive Insurance (800-776-4737, www.progressive.com/myrate) in Kentucky, Michigan, Minnesota, New Jersey, and Oregon. In order to participate, you must install a device (sent to you free by the company) in your car that tracks mileage. The company then reviews the collected information and lets you know how much of a discount you're entitled to. The discount is based on how much you drive, how aggressively you drive, and when you drive.

$ TIP Take time to browse Progressive's Web site; it has detailed information on other ways to cut auto insurance premiums that may apply to your situation.

GMAC (877-469-5619, www.lowmileagediscount.com) has a similar program, available in 34 states, for GM cars that are equipped with the OnStar navigation system. You can save up to 54% on premiums if you drive less than 15,000 miles annually.

ANNUAL MILEAGE	AVERAGE TOTAL SAVINGS
0–2,500	54%
2,501–5,000	39%
5,001–7,500	34%
7,501–10,000	26%
10,001–12,500	18%
12,501–15,000	13%

Note: Unlike Progressive's plan, GMAC tracks only mileage and not when you drive or how aggressively you drive.

About Homeowners Insurance

Although there are fewer ways to save here than on your car insurance, take time to run through this checklist.

16. INSTALL SECURITY. Smoke detectors, burglar alarms, or deadbolt locks are key. Savings: 5 to 10%. Add a fire and burglar alarm that's connected to a third-party monitoring service and you could save from 15 to 25%.

17. DON'T SMOKE. Some insurers offer discounts for nonsmoking households. Savings: Up to 5%.

18. DEDUCTIBLES MATTER TOO. The standard deductible is $500, so you'll get a discount if you opt for a higher deductible of $1,000. Savings: Up to 25%.

19. SPEAK UP IF YOU HAVE SOMETHING NEW. Brand new homes and even those five to ten years old usually mean cheaper premiums. And let your company know if your house's wiring, plumbing, and heating systems have been installed in the past ten years. Savings: Up to 15%.

20. TELL YOUR AGE. Homeowners over age 55 are often eligible for discounts. Savings: Up to 15%.

A Few More Ways to Save

INSURE ONLY YOUR HOME. Your house is what's covered by homeowner's insurance, not your entire property. So consider only the value of your home when deciding on the amount of your coverage.

THINK ABOUT YOUR DOG. Insurers may charge more if you own a "more aggressive" breed (rottweilers, pit bulls, German shepherds), or they may require you to carry pricier umbrella coverage.

SKIP FLOATERS YOU NO LONGER NEED. If you donated your fabulous fur to a charity, gave you daughter your Sheffield tea set, or handed over your coin collection to your nephew, cancel your floater.

THE BOTTOM LINE: As you work on paying your bills and living within a budget, keep in mind the words on a sign in an Arkansas diner: "In God we trust. All others pay cash!"

WORDSMARTS

DEDUCTIBLE: The amount of loss paid for by the insurance policyholder. It can be a specific dollar amount or a percentage of the claim. For example, if your deductible is $500 and you have $800 worth of damage, the insurance company will cover $300 and you'll pay $500 out of pocket. Note: The bigger the deductible, the lower the premium you'll be charged for the same coverage.

FIXED EXPENSES: Those household expenses that cannot be changed (or changed very much), such as rent, mortgage payments, and utilities.

FLOATER: Attached to a homeowner's policy, a floater insures movable property, covering losses wherever they occur. A floater is most often used to cover expensive jewelry, furs, musical instruments, computers, printers, fax machines, and the like.

INSURANCE PREMIUMS: The payments, usually made on a regular periodic basis, that a policyholder must make to an insurance company in order to own her policy.

VARIABLE EXPENSES: Those household expenses that can be changed (either increased or decreased), such as restaurant dining, travel, entertainment, and luxury items.

FOR FURTHER INFORMATION

"**INSURANCE BASICS**" and many other useful publications are free from the Insurance Information Institute, www.iii.org.

"**66 WAYS TO SAVE MONEY ON EVERYTHING**" is available from the Federal Citizen Information Center (888-878-3256, www.pueblo. gsa.gov/cic_text/money/66ways/index.html).

4

Tapping into Your Assets: When You Run Out of Cash

"Neither a borrower, nor a lender be,
For loan oft loses both itself and friend."
—SHAKESPEARE, *HAMLET*, ACT I, SCENE 3

Sometimes we simply run out of cash. It might be because we were careless and spent too much. But it also could happen if you lose your job. You could have huge medical bills. Your business could fail despite your hard work. You may have invested in a hedge fund that went under. Your 401(k) may have tanked because of a bear market or because the company you work for went bankrupt. Now and then, even the most fiscally conservative need cash in a flash. Here are a myriad of choices.

Many people react to a lack of money by ignoring the fact, burying their head in the sand because of personal embarrassment. This, of course, only makes matters worse. If it's any consolation, you're in good company. Over the years, a number of famous people have run out of cash. One of the earliest documented cases was that of Edward III, King of England. Instead of being happy with running his own country, he got greedy and set out to conquer France as well. This led to the start of the Hundred Years' War in 1337, which in turn forced Edward into bankruptcy. The amount involved was £30,000, an enormous sum in 1340.

Financial disaster can happen to the rich and powerful or the brilliant and talented. Charles Goodyear's experiments led to a process for vulcanizing rubber, but he was such a poor businessman that when he died in 1860, he left his family $200,000 in debt. James Abbott McNeill Whistler, one of our greatest painters, lived a lavish lifestyle that often tossed him into debt. He took offense at a review by art critic John Ruskin and sued him for libel. The cost of the lawsuit sent him into bankruptcy in 1879. Mark Twain, the brilliant author of *Tom Sawyer*, declared bankruptcy in 1894 because of bad investments. And then there was Phineas Taylor Barnum. He overextended himself in real estate, and an especially ill-advised investment in the Jerome Clock Company sent him into bankruptcy. He then bounced back and founded Barnum and Bailey's Circus. In more recent times, Walt Disney, Debbie Reynolds, Larry King, and Donald Trump have all filed for bankruptcy at one time or another in their lives.

But what about you? You and your accountant should review the following options. I can't specify which should be your number one choice. That depends on what assets you own, where they are, and how much they're worth.

SECURED VERSUS UNSECURED LOANS

Before you get a loan, bear in mind that *secured loans* are cheaper than *unsecured loans*. Secured loans are backed by an asset or assets, such as stocks, bonds, Treasuries, bank CDs, savings accounts, retirement accounts, real estate, or other properties.

Unsecured loans are basically signature loans and are granted by banks, credit unions, credit card issuers, and family members and friends.

Rates on unsecured loans are higher than those on secured loans.

$ TIP After you read this chapter and before you take out a loan, go to www.dinkytown.net and run your numbers through the loan comparison calculators. Then you'll have a clear picture of the costs involved with various types of loans.

PERSONAL LOANS

It's a well-known fact that more often that not, finances and friendship do not mix well. In fact, loans from family members and friends have a high default risk. However, such a loan need not rupture a relationship if you handle it in a businesslike manner.

As Samuel Goldwyn, founder of Metro-Goldwyn-Mayer, pointed out, "A verbal contract isn't worth the paper it's printed on." So, set up a formal written plan, including the amount of the loan, a repayment schedule, and the interest rate—just as a banker would. You can use a promissory note, available at stationery stores or downloadable from www.lawdepot.com. You both should sign and date the document.

$ TIP Be sure the friend or relative you ask is in a position to loan you money and that you are in a position to pay it back.

Refrain from asking for money at a social or family gathering. Not only might you ruin your friend's cocktail party or your family's Thanksgiving dinner, but you're putting your friend or relative on the spot with other people around. Instead, make an appointment to discuss your financial situation. At that meeting, spell out how much you need to borrow, why, for how long, and where you will get the money to pay back the loan. And, explain that you will pay interest. (In determining the interest rate, use prime as a benchmark. Your rate can be slightly above or below prime, depending upon your lender's wishes.)

COMMERCIAL LOANS

Banks, credit unions, and even brokerage firms are all in the business of selling cash. To find the best deal, study the information given here, conquer the jargon, and follow Steps 1 through 4. Remember, the shorter the length of the loan, the higher the monthly payment but the lower the total cost.

STEP 1. CALL YOUR BANK FIRST. Banks and credit unions often give lower rates and faster approval for their own customers.

STEP 2. COMPARISON SHOP. Rates and terms very widely, even among banks in the same town. Set aside some telephone and online time to gather the facts. You can also check out rates at www.bankrate.com.

STEP 3. GO FOR A SECURED LOAN FIRST. If you put up collateral, the interest rate will be lower than with an unsecured loan—one based merely on your signature.

STEP 4. BE AWARE OF CURRENT INTEREST-RATE TRENDS. Many loan rates are not fixed, but instead are adjustable, moving up and down with the Treasury bill rate, the prime rate, or some other official rate. If you take out an adjustable loan, make certain that you can handle future rate increases.

Secured Loans

Your bank or credit union may lend you money using your savings account or CD as collateral, charging 2 to 3% more than the rate you are being paid on these very same deposits. If you fail to pay off this type of secured loan, the bank will deduct both the principal and the interest from your deposit.

$ TIP If you're very self-disciplined, skip the loan and withdraw money from your savings account, paying it back as soon as possible. In effect, you're borrowing from yourself.

A word about cashing in a CD before maturity: you'll be slapped with an early withdrawal penalty, which could be as much as 30 to 90 days of interest on a one-year CD, with penalties rising for longer-term certificates. On the other hand, doing so might be wise if it covers your shortfall. It means you won't be running up additional debt.

Unsecured Loans

If you don't have collateral, you may still be able to get an unsecured bank loan (or a credit card loan; see the later discussion) on your signature alone. Of course, you'll have to pay a higher interest rate. Unsecured lines of credit at banks and credit unions allow you to access from $1,000 to $100,000 by writing a check. The amount you qualify for depends on your income and your credit rating. Most such loans have a fixed rate of interest (14 to 15%) and allow one to five years to repay.

You can also tap into a cash advance on your Visa, Master-Card, or almost any other bank card by simply writing a check (supplied by the credit card company) or putting your card into an ATM machine. It's easy, and it feels totally painless.

But watch out. These loans are extremely seductive and should be used only in an emergency until you can negotiate a better deal elsewhere. The cost is high, with rates ranging from 18 to 24%. In addition, many card issuers also charge a transaction fee, which could be up to 4% of the total loan.

REAL ESTATE LOANS

Because interest on consumer loans (those just described) is not tax-deductible and interest on real estate loans generally is, it may make sense for you to borrow against the value of your home or co-op. But such loans should only be for important purposes and not for vacations or luxury items.

There are two such types of loans. One is the old-fashioned *second mortgage* (now called a *home equity loan*), which is a closed-end loan in which you borrow a fixed amount all at once and repay it in monthly installments over a set period, such as 10 years. Interest is more often than not also fixed.

The other type of real estate loan is the *home equity line of credit* (HELOC), in which you borrow money (using specially issued checks or a credit card) as you need it against a maximum established when you open the account. The interest rate is usually variable.

Most lenders will give you 85% of the appraised value of the house, minus what you owe on it. The amount also depends on your income.

! CAUTION A great many Americans refinance their homes to pay down their debts—most often credit card debts, but sometimes education loans. It's true that in most cases, you are getting rid of high-interest debt and replacing it with lower-interest debt, yet it's a risky move. You are also reducing the equity in your home. If you lose your job or face a serious illness and can't make your loan payments, your house could be repossessed (see Chapter 6 on foreclosures).

$ TIP Keep in mind that your house can also be turned into a source of immediate cash if you take in a boarder or roommate or rent out space you don't need, such as your garage, barn, or a shed.

COMPANY LOANS

Don't overlook your employer. Many companies have systems in place to help employees who are in need of loans. The interest rate is typically prime or slightly more.

! CAUTION Do not confuse this type of loan with what's known as a payday loan, in which you borrow against your next paycheck. You've probably seen or heard these loans advertised: "Need cash until your next payday? Get $50 to $500 within 15 minutes. No credit check!" They're also called "check loans" and "payroll advance loans," and they are made by private loan companies.

These loans are not a wise move—if you don't pay back the loan, it may be automatically renewed with yet more fees and interest. Here's an example from the Federal Trade Commission:

> *You need to borrow $100 for two weeks. You write a personal check for $115, with $15 being the fee to borrow the money. The payday lender agrees to hold your check until your next payday. When that day comes around, either the lender deposits the check and you redeem it by paying the $115 in cash, or you roll over the loan and are charged $15 more to extend the financing for 14 more days. If you agree to electronic payments instead of a check, on your next payday the company debits the full amount of the loan from your checking account electronically or extends the loan for an additional $15. The cost of the initial $100 loan is a $15 finance charge and an annual percentage rate of 391%. If you roll over the loan three times, the finance charge would climb to $60 to borrow the $100.*

$ TIP If you're tempted by loans of this kind, be sure to read the rest of the FTC's warning at www.ftc.gov. Click on "Consumer Information."

401(k) LOANS

Well over half of all firms allow their employees to tap into their 401(k) plan. Check with your administrator for specifics. There are two ways in which you can dip into your 401(k): via a financial hardship withdrawal or via a loan. Of the two, as you will see, a loan is preferable, but both types of loans come with serious minuses.

Unless you've exhausted all other sources of money, don't dip into your retirement savings.

401(k) Hardship Withdrawals

The IRS allows financial hardship loans for very narrow and specific reasons. They are

- To pay for unreimbursed medical expenses, but only for you or your dependents
- To prevent foreclosure on your home (or eviction)
- To buy a primary residence
- To pay college tuition (and approved related education costs) for you or a dependent

But a hardship withdrawal is not an automatic thing. First of all, individual employers can impose tougher restrictions, or they can completely bar such withdrawals. The negatives regarding hardship withdrawals are

- You must pay income tax on the entire amount that you take out.

- If you are under age 59½, you must also pay a 10% early withdrawal penalty, with rare exceptions.
- You'll be asked personal questions about why you need the money. Many employers insist that you prove that you've exhausted all other sources of money.
- You will be giving up part of a key asset. Federal law protects your 401(k) from creditors. So if you were to file for personal bankruptcy or go into foreclosure, your 401(k) would be safe.

Finally, you're obviously depleting money that has been specifically set aside for your retirement.

Now that we've laid out the pertinent details about a hardship withdrawal, let's look at the plain 401(k) loan.

401(k) Loans

Most plans allow employees to borrow up to $50,000 or 50% of the amount invested in the plan, whichever is less. And the interest rate is low, compared with those for other types of loans—typically 1 or 2 percentage points above prime. And, you'll have five years in which to pay back the loan.

Again, you're obviously depleting money that was set aside for your retirement. The growth of your 401(k) is directly hampered by the amount you take out.

Equally important is the fact that if you leave your job or are fired, you must repay the loan, and fairly quickly. Most plans insist upon repayment within 30 to 90 days after your final day of work. If you don't repay the money, you will be hit with taxes on the outstanding dollar amount.

$ TIP You'll find a wealth of material at www.401khelpcenter.com.

PROS: Your payments are made back into your own retirement account, not to a bank. These payments are automatically deducted from your paycheck, so you won't miss payments.

CONS: The amount you take out reduces both the amount you have saved for retirement and the amount available for tax-free compounding. This is especially true if your employer matches your contributions. And the interest paid, unlike that on real estate loans, is not tax-deductible.

You'll also be taxed twice on the loan amount. The money that you take out is money that you contributed to the plan before taxes. But you're paying it back with after-tax money. Then, when you withdraw the money upon retirement, it will be taxed yet again.

IRA LOANS

Unlike the situation with 401(k) plans, you can withdraw money from your individual retirement account at any time. But you'll be hit with taxes—federal taxes on your withdrawals and, if you're under age 59½, an additional 10% early withdrawal penalty.

There are several situations, however, in which you can take money out of your IRA without paying the 10% early withdrawal penalty, although you'll still have to pay taxes:

- To buy or rebuild a first home
- To pay for qualified higher education costs for you, your spouse, or your children or grandchildren

- If you become disabled, as defined by the IRS
- If your unreimbursed medical payments are more than 7.5% of your adjusted gross income
- To pay for medical insurance when you're unemployed

If you are considering a loan to buy a first home, keep in mind that due to the 2009 stimulus plan, first-time home buyers are eligible for an $8,000 tax credit, provided they purchase their primary residence by December 1, 2009. (This cutoff date may be extended.) The credit does not need to be repaid unless you sell your home within three years. The credit phases out for taxpayers whose adjusted gross income exceeds $75,000 or $150,000 for married couples.

$ TIP Once a year, you can borrow money without paying anything to the IRS—as long as you put the money back within 60 days. But if you miss the deadline, the full amount of the loan will be considered as taxable income.

LIFE INSURANCE LOANS

If you have a cash value–type insurance policy, you'll probably be able to borrow 75 to 90% of its cash value. Rates are usually very low, you're not required to give a reason, and you'll receive a check within two weeks or less.

Although you are not required to pay back the loan, you obviously should do so when your financial crisis has passed. The original purpose of the policy was to protect your family. Should you die while the loan is still outstanding, the policy's death benefit will be reduced by the amount of the loan.

MARGIN ACCOUNT LOANS

If you have a brokerage account, read on. You can get a loan from your stockbroker by setting up a special margin account and using your securities as collateral.

You could also simply sell your securities and use the cash. However, if you want to keep your portfolio intact and avoid capital gains taxes, think about a margin account, but with the greatest of care.

The interest rate on this type of secured loan is based on the broker call rate, the rate that banks charge brokers when they lend them money. The interest your broker then charges you typically runs from 0.5 to 3% above the broker loan rate. This interest can be deducted from your investment income on your 1040.

The Federal Reserve Board allows stockbrokers to make loans of up to 95% of the value of U.S. Treasuries and up to 50% of the value of stocks in a customer's account. Many brokers set even more stringent requirements.

Sounds great. But there are high risks attached. If the value of your portfolio falls below a minimum amount, you'll receive a *margin call* from your broker, meaning that you must come up with enough collateral to keep the loan. If you are short of cash and cannot do this, then your broker will sell enough of your remaining securities to meet the call. And, of course, this call comes at the worst time possible: when your securities are tumbling in price.

$ TIP To fully understand the pros and cons of this type of account, read "Margin Trading" on the Securities and Exchange Commission Web site at www.sec.gov/investor/pubs/margin.htm.

OTHER WAYS TO RAISE CASH

If you don't need a huge amount of money to carry you over to your next paycheck or your next job, why not sell things you don't need? Hold a garage sale, take them to a consignment shop, or sell them on eBay or a similar site. You could also place ads in local newspapers and on various community bulletin boards. Really valuable items should be placed in an auction.

Among the items you might get cash for are

Athletic equipment	*Games*
Boats	*Jewelry*
Books	*Paintings*
Clothing	*Silver items*
Dishes	*Small appliances*
Furniture	*Toys*
	Vehicles

WordSmarts

BROKER LOAN RATE: The interest rate at which brokers borrow money from banks.

CASH VALUE: The dollar amount you may borrow against a life insurance policy. Part of your insurance payments or premiums is used to buy death benefits, and part goes into an investment account that pays a fixed or variable rate of return. The money in the investment account is what can be borrowed.

COLLATERAL: The property or asset pledged as security for a loan, such as a bank savings account or CDs, securities, or real estate. If the borrower defaults, the lender can sell the collateral and use the proceeds to satisfy the remaining debt.

EQUITY: The amount of property you own outright; it's based on the fair market value minus any outstanding principal due—on your mortgage in the case of real estate.

MARGIN LOAN: A loan from a brokerage firm collateralized by the securities in a special margin account.

PRIME RATE: The interest rate that a bank charges its top-rated commercial borrowers.

SECURED LOAN: A loan that is backed or secured by something tangible, such as real estate, savings accounts, securities, or a car.

TREASURIES: IOU-type investments issued by the federal government and sold to individuals and institutions. All Treasuries pay interest that is free from state but not federal income taxes. Treasury bills mature (come due) within one year, Treasury notes mature in one to ten years, and Treasury bonds mature in ten years or more. Along with EE savings bonds, Treasuries are the safest of investments because they are backed by the U.S. government.

UNSECURED LOAN: A loan that is not backed by a tangible asset; also known as a signature loan. Credit card loans are unsecured.

VESTED: The amount that an employee has a right to receive from the benefits contributed to a pension plan by that employee or his employer. This nonforfeitable dollar amount belongs to the employee even if he changes jobs, retires, or is fired. The length of time it takes to become fully vested varies, with five years being typical.

FOR FURTHER INFORMATION

SOLVE YOUR MONEY PROBLEMS, by Robin Leonard, 11th ed. (Berkeley, Calif.: Nolo Press, 2007).

HOW TO BE THE FAMILY CFO, by Kim Snider (Austin, Tex.: Greenleaf Book Group, 2008).

5

Ramping Up Your Savings

"The safest way to double your money is to fold it over once and put it in your pocket."

—FRANK MCKINNEY HUBBARD

If only it were as easy as the late Mr. Hubbard, an American cartoonist, humorist, and journalist, says. It takes more than folding techniques to save money—you need discipline and, of course, sources of money. In this chapter you'll find both.

21 PAINLESS WAYS TO SAVE

The rule of thumb is: save six or, better yet, nine months of living expenses. (The average time for finding a new job is currently a little over four months.) Then, if you lose your job, become ill, or for some other reason are not working, you have money to tide you over. Very logical. The nest egg should be in a safe interest-bearing account or an insured bank CD.

Here are 21 ways to fill your nest egg. You may not become "as rich as Croesus," but you'll be on your way.

Croesus, incidentally, was not a mythological character. He lived in ancient Lydia, now Turkey, during the sixth century BCE and was in fact the last king of Lydia. Croesus arguably might have fared better if he had avoided the Oracle at Delphi, who told him: "You shall destroy a powerful nation." Croesus took this to mean that he would conquer one; instead, he lost his own country to the Persians!

But what Croesus lacked in military skill, he more than made up for in business and financial acumen. He conservatively managed his assets—wealth from the conquests made by his father, Alyattes II; profits from savvy trading deals; and a savings nest egg that consisted largely of gold. He even paved the way for future banking and commerce by inventing the first formal currency system, minting both gold and silver coins.

Personal Strategies

1. SET PERSONAL GOALS. Just as your goal on the tennis court, golf course, or chessboard is to win, so it should be with savings. Identify a specific goal, such as build my savings account to $XXX by December 31, save enough to purchase a car or start my own business, or have enough money on hand by the beginning of June for a summer vacation. Then mark down how much you need to save each week or month to fund your goal. Having specifics in mind makes saving a much more focused and meaningful task.

2. THINK SMALL. The classic mistake most people make is thinking that they don't have enough money to save. If you believe that nonsense, you will talk yourself into doing absolutely nothing, which translates into saving absolutely nothing.

Don't go down that path. Any amount saved is an amount saved, and small amounts earning interest add up, just not as fast as larger amounts. If you need convincing, study the "Rule of 72" box later in this chapter.

3. TREAT YOUR SAVINGS LIKE A MONTHLY BILL. Put aside money before you spend it. Once a month, when you pay your bills, write out a check (or arrange for an automatic deposit) to go into your savings account. Make it the second check you write—the first being your rent or your mortgage.

Begin by saving 1% of your take-home pay the first month and increase the amount by 1% each month. At the end of 12 months, you'll be saving 12% of your take-home pay. If you can afford it, double or triple the percentage you are socking away.

4. CALL YOUR BANK. Direct it to transfer a specific sum from your checking account into savings or a money market account on a monthly basis.

5. KEEP ON MAKING REGULAR PAYMENTS. After you pay off a car or college loan, your mortgage, or other debts, continue to write a check for the same amount, or at least half the amount, and stash it in your savings account. You have been living without that money each month for several years and maybe longer, so saving it should be relatively easy. Switching debt for savings is a painless way to stockpile dollars.

6. SAVE YOUR CHANGE AT THE END OF EACH DAY. You've probably given this advice to your children, suggesting that they put pennies in their piggy bank or a mayonnaise jar. You might try the same strategy, but instead of pennies, save quarters or dollar bills.

$ TIP Save $5 at the end of each day and you'll have $35 a week or $140 a month. That might be enough "bridge money" to get you to your next paycheck without having to use a credit card.

Other Possibilities

7. DIVIDENDS. Reinvest the dividends you receive from stocks or, if you prefer, take the dividends as cash and put them into savings, but never spend them.

8. TAX REFUNDS. Whether they are from your local, state, or federal taxing authorities, don't fritter the money away on unnecessary items.

9. ATMS. Every time you use an ATM within your own bank's system, you save money. For instance, if you're in the habit of using the ATM in the lobby of your office building or at your neighborhood grocery store, and it's not part of your bank's network, you could be paying several dollars in fees—often to both banks—with each and every transaction. Instead, make a point of using only your own bank's ATMs. Then put the amount you saved in your mayonnaise jar at the end of the day.

10. INSURANCE REIMBURSEMENTS. If you have already covered your expenses without the reimbursement, when the check comes in, put all or half of it into savings.

11. SALE ITEMS. If you buy something on sale, put the rest of the full price into savings.

12. CASH GIFTS. If someone gives you cash or a check for a special occasion, such as your birthday, graduation, or the like, add it to your account.

13. GAMING WINNINGS. If you hit it big at the casino, walk away with your winnings and add them to your savings.

> **! CAUTION** All gambling winnings are fully taxable. This includes not only cash prizes but also the fair market value of noncash items, such as cars or trips. For more details, check IRS Publication 525, "Taxable and Nontaxable Income," which you can download at www.irs.gov. Bear in mind that if you itemize, you can deduct gambling losses as a miscellaneous deduction—but only up to the amount of gambling income reported.

14. SILLINESS. When you spend money on something frivolous or nonessential, put that same amount into savings.

Work-Related Strategies

15. BUY EE SAVINGS BONDS. Many companies have an automatic plan so that employees can purchase these ultra-safe bonds, backed by the U.S. government. You never see the money, as it's funneled out of your paycheck. Bonds sell for as little as $25 if purchased electronically, or $50 for a paper certificate. Your firm, however, may have a higher monthly minimum.

The interest rate, which is based on the average market yield on five-year Treasury notes for the previous six months, changes every May 1 and November 1. As we go to press, the rate on bonds issued through April 30, 2009, is 1.30%. (This interest is exempt from state and local taxes.)

Note: You can also purchase Series EE bonds online through the TreasuryDirect system (www.savingsbonds.gov) or at your bank. TreasuryDirect also has a great FAQ section that covers a number of topics, including bond safety and tax implications. An alternative that gives you a hedge against future inflation is Series I bonds, with I standing for inflation. These too can be purchased electronically for as little as $25, or for just $50 if you are buying paper certificates. The interest rate, a combination of a fixed rate plus an inflation rate that is adjusted twice a year, is 5.64% through April 30, 2009.

16. SIGN UP FOR YOUR COMPANY'S PAYROLL DEDUCTION PLAN. Your employer may offer a payroll deduction or direct deposit plan as a way to help employees save. You designate how much money you want automatically deducted from your paycheck and put in a savings account or money market fund. [There are no tax advantages here, as there are with a 401(k) plan.]

Most credit unions and banks accept deposits from a firm's payroll department. The transfer is made electronically, so you won't miss it and it starts earning interest almost at once.

17. PARTICIPATE IN A STOCK PURCHASE PLAN. Some companies offer employees the opportunity to buy the company's stock with pretax dollars, often at a discount from the current market price. It's generally done through payroll withholding.

You do not pay taxes on the value of the stock until you leave the company. In the interim, if the stock increases in value, it does so on a tax-deferred basis. If you sell the stock, any discount you received is taxed as regular income. Profits may be taxed at the more favorable long-term capital gains rates, depending on how long you held the stock.

18. FIND OUT ABOUT ANY PROFIT-SHARING PLAN. Another way some companies link compensation to the fortunes of the firm is through profit-sharing plans. Typically, employees are given a part of the firm's profits as a quarterly or year-end cash bonus. The funds may be held in trust by the company until you leave the firm or retire. Some companies allow employees to add voluntary contributions. Taxes on the contributions made by the company and all the earnings in the account are deferred until the money is withdrawn.

19. FLEXIBLE SPENDING PLANS SOMETIMES REIMBURSE PARTICIPANTS. If you're that lucky, put the reimbursement into savings.

20. BONUSES ARE JUST THAT. If you receive a bonus for a job well done at work or a traditional holiday or year-end one, put it right into savings. It's money you were not counting on, so it's money that easily can be parked in savings.

21. SAVE HALF OF "SURPRISE" EARNINGS. If you have taken on a freelance project or a temporary assignment, or if you are making money helping someone for a few hours a week, make a point of saving half of this extra income.

THE BOTTOM LINE: Make savings a game, a personal challenge. At the end of each week, see how much you have left from your weekly budget. And then save that entire amount.

THE RULE OF 72

The classic "Rule of 72" calculates how long it will take to double your money, regardless of the interest rate. All you do is divide 72 by the interest rate. The result is the number of years it takes to double your savings.

For example:

72 divided by 3½% is 20½ years

72 divided by 6% is 12 years

NOTE: This rule applies only when interest and dividends are reinvested and does not take taxes into consideration.

WORDSMARTS

ATM: Automatic teller machine. These network machines enable customers to perform banking activities even when a bank is closed. Services offered vary but always include withdrawing cash.

STOCK DIVIDEND: Usually but not always cash payments made to a company's shareholders. Dividends are a distribution of profits to the owners of the company.

STOCK PURCHASE PLAN: Plan through which a corporation's employees become partial owners. Unlike other retirement plans, contributions must be invested in the company's stocks. Employees get to share in the company's success while employers hope for increased productivity from involved workers. Also called ESOP (Employee Stock Ownership Plan).

FOR FURTHER INFORMATION

CONSUMER ACTION HANDBOOK. An annual published by the Federal Citizen Information Center. For a free copy call: 888-878-3256 or visit: www.consumeraction.gov.

PERSONAL FINANCE FOR DUMMIES, 5th ed., by Eric Tyson (IDG Books Worldwide, Inc.).

6

Fighting Foreclosure and Higher Property Taxes

"Chance favors only the prepared mind."
—LOUIS PASTEUR

Being prepared and knowing the facts about your mortgage and your property taxes gives you significant leverage—for negotiating both your way out of foreclosure and lower real estate taxes. You don't want to lose your home or pay a whopping tax bill. Here's how to come out on top in both situations.

FIGHTING BACK

On the evening of December 16, 1773, members of the Sons of Liberty, a political group, many of them disguised as Mohawk Indians, boarded three ships in Boston Harbor. In an orderly and quiet manner, they broke open the tea chests and dumped an estimated 10,000 pounds' worth (roughly $1 million today) of Darjeeling into the sea. It was their way of protesting against the onerous British tax policies.

Because the Bostonians refused to pay for the destroyed tea, the British Parliament passed the Coercive Acts of 1774, which, among other things, closed the city's port. This move outraged the colonists and sparked tax rebellions up and down the East Coast.

John Adams, who rarely favored mob action, wrote about the event: "There is a dignity, a majesty, a sublimity, in this last effort of the patriots that I greatly admire."

His words ought to give you courage—to fight foreclosure proceedings and challenge your real estate tax bill.

FORECLOSURES

Facing Mortgage Problems Up Front

You've seen the numbers. They're stunningly negative, with thousands of Americans having had their homes repossessed. And foreclosures continue to loom for those who are unable to make their current payments as a result of unemployment or other financial reverses.

If you are falling behind on your mortgage, or fear you will, read on. There are solutions.

Type of Loan

Your first step is to find your mortgage document. Then, if you have difficulty reading financial papers, ask a knowledgeable friend or your accountant to read it with you. Here's what to look for:

- Do you have an adjustable-rate loan? If so, how often can the rate be raised? What is the maximum to which it can be raised? What is the current rate?

- If you have a fixed-rate loan, what is the rate?
- Can you pay off your loan early? If the answer is yes, is there a penalty for doing so? And, when does the penalty expire?
- Who is your contact person?

Contacting Your Lender

Once you have gathered this information, if you anticipate falling behind in making payments (or if you have already done so), contact your lender immediately. You'll find the telephone number on your monthly statement. Don't delay doing so by one month, one week, or even one day. Lenders who never hear from those with payment problems are forced to take legal action, which can result in foreclosure. In fact, once you are three or more months behind, your lender will give your loan to an attorney, who in turn will initiate foreclosure proceedings. At this point, you will be in serious danger of losing your home.

Calling your lender, in fact, is absolutely the most important thing you can do. Lenders are in the money business, not the real estate business. They would rather help you keep your home than get stuck with a problem piece of property that they will then need to unload. The vast majority, in fact, will help you come up with a solution.

$ TIP If you think about the situation from the lender's viewpoint—that it doesn't want to wind up with your house—this should give you courage and mental leverage for negotiating a solution.

If you're nervous or uncomfortable about talking to your lender (most understandable), contact a nonprofit mortgage counseling agency—but only one certified by the U.S. Department of Housing and Urban Development (HUD). To find one in your area, call 800-569-4287 or visit www.hud.gov/fore closure. Counselors will help you develop a plan to avoid foreclosure for free or at minimal cost.

Also check with the Home Ownership Preservation Foundation at 888-995-HOPE, www.hopenow.com. Known as HOPE, this organization also helps homeowners remain in their homes and provides free credit counseling.

Your lender will want to know if your financial crunch is temporary (you're out of work for a while, but you will be able to make regular payments once you find a job, or you've had a major illness or injury but will be able to return to full-time work within a few months) or if it's a longer-term problem (you have a permanent disability; you are unable to pay your bills; your credit cards are maxed out and you owe huge debts). Be honest—you may be asked to document the reason you're having difficulty paying your mortgage.

Before making that first phone call, however, it's wise to have a concrete plan in mind. For example, work out the dollar amount that you can afford to pay every month and ask your lender if that amount would be acceptable. If you've lost your job, reassure the lender that you are actively looking for a new one. Or tell him that you will be taking on a part-time position, or that your spouse is working or plans to work.

Among the loan modification options that the lender (or you) might raise are

- A lower interest rate (permanent or temporary)
- Extending the length of the mortgage (possibly to 40 years)
- Smaller monthly payments

- Deferral of principal (often at zero interest)
- Making up missed payments via a plan devised specifically for you

Keep a log of all conversations with your lender, including the names of the people you speak with, the dates, and a summary of the comments made. And keep copies of all e-mails and written correspondence.

$ TIP The American Recover and Reinvestment Act that went into effect in February 2009 is designed to help millions of financially struggling homeowners keep their homes. Various aspects of the plan allow homeowners to reduce mortgage payments or refinance through government-backed refinancing arrangements. Don't forget to ask your lender if you qualify.

DOCUMENTS THAT YOUR LENDER MAY WANT

Before calling your lender to negotiate a loan modification, line up these documents:

- Your net worth statement (see Chapter 1)

- Your monthly expenses

- Unemployment records

- Paycheck stubs

- Social security statement

- Your last tax return

Note: In some cases, lenders ask homeowners to write and sign a "hardship letter" explaining their situation.

Solutions That Go beyond Your Lender

If your lender won't budge, your next step is to get outside assistance.

If you have an FHA-secured loan, contact the Department of Housing and Urban Development at 800-255-5342, www.hud.gov/foreclosure/index.cfm, for details on how to stay (or get) out of foreclosure.

Even if you don't have an FHA mortgage, the FHA may be able to help by converting your loan to a more affordable government-backed mortgage through the HOPE for Homeowners Program (H4H): 800-225-5342, www.hud.gov/hopeforhome owners. The H4H program runs through September 2011.

If you're a veteran, check with the Veterans Administration for information on the Veterans' Benefits Improvement Act of 2008: 877-827-3702, www.homeloans.va.gov. It enables vets to convert subprime loans and ARMs to guaranteed VA loans.

The Mortgage Bankers Association (www.homeloanlearn ingcenter.com) has consumer information and links to helpful resources. Click on "Foreclosure Prevention Resource Center" on the right.

RENTING

Here are three possible renting solutions.

1. RENT YOUR HOUSE TO AN INDIVIDUAL. Obviously this works only if you can live elsewhere or you have a large enough house to share with a renter.

2. TURN YOUR HOUSE INTO A SHORT-TERM CORPORATE RENTAL. A number of companies have substantial budgets for helping executives who are relocating or employees who regularly travel on business. Your rental income is likely to be considerably higher than when renting directly to an individual.

Check with www.corporatehousingbyowner.com for more information.

3. RENT BACK YOUR FORECLOSED HOUSE. Freddie Mac has a new plan that allows homeowners to stay in homes by renting them back once the home has been acquired by Freddie Mac through foreclosure. This gives you time to find a new place to live. You are required to pay market-value rent but no mortgage payments.

A Short Sale

In the final analysis, if you cannot renegotiate the terms of your mortgage and cannot find a renter and, at the same time, your home is now worth less than you owe, you may want to consider what is known as a *short sale*. Your lender, of course, will need to grant approval for this solution.

In a short sale, you sell your home to a new buyer at an agreed-upon price, and your lender then forgives the remaining amount due on your mortgage.

This enables you to get out of your mortgage without foreclosure and without filing for bankruptcy. *Note:* A foreclosure remains on your credit report for seven years, while bankruptcy is there for ten years. Both make it more difficult for you to get a mortgage in the future.

A short sale also enables the buyer of your home to purchase it at a good price, and your lender isn't left with a difficult-to-sell piece of property.

However, a short sale might affect your credit score, depending on how it appears on your credit report. You should talk to your lender about reporting the sale in the least negative manner possible.

$ TIP Under the Mortgage Forgiveness Debt Relief Act of 2007, signed by President Bush in late 2007, sellers are no longer required to pay taxes on the amount of debt forgiven in a short sale. This protective piece of legislation is in effect through 2012. It applies to mortgage restructuring and debt forgiveness in connection with foreclosure on a principal residence for amounts up to $2 million ($1 million if you file a separate tax return).

10 Ways to Refinance When No One Is Lending

It's tough refinancing these days. Banks are legitimately nervous because of recent industry failures and their own foolhardy practices, which led to the need for bailouts. Add in declining property values, the increasing number of foreclosures, and the rising unemployment rate, and it's understandable that lenders worry about which of their customers might not be able to make their loan payments.

It should come as no surprise, then, that refinancing rules have been tightened. There's no more merely signing on the dotted line. To refinance at the best rates available, mortgage lenders now require a credit score of 720 or better, and they also want to see that you have at least 20% equity (the difference between what an owner owes on a mortgage and the appraised worth of the property) in your house.

Here are 10 ways to improve the likelihood you can refinance. Ideally, at least one of them will work for you.

1. KNOW YOUR LENDER. Pay your mortgage on time. Then stay in touch with the mortgage representative at your bank, and keep the name of that person on file. Ask if you can call (or stop in) to discuss new rates and options, or if she will add you to an e-mail list to keep you posted. Maintaining a personal relationship doesn't guarantee that you can refinance, but it will give you a little extra edge and help the bank to know you as a person rather than an application.

2. CONSIDER OTHER LENDERS. While you want to start with your current lender, check other sources. Smaller community banks kept themselves somewhat removed from the world of mortgage-backed securities, so many of them have the best rates and availability right now. In addition, ask friends and neighbors for recommendations of local bankers, and check rates online. Then go back to your current lender and ask if he can match what you found elsewhere.

3. CLOSE DOWN A SECOND LOAN. Your fiscal appearance counts. If you have an untapped line of credit (known as a home equity loan), tell your lender that you would like it terminated.

4. UPDATE YOUR INCOME INFORMATION IF IT'S INCREASED. If you've taken on a second job, your spouse is now working, or you've come into an inheritance, present documentation of these facts to your lender. Other sources of an improved bottom line since your original mortgage might include: rental income, bonuses, royalties, annuities, and limited partnership payouts, as well as bonds, bank CDs, and savings bonds coming due and required minimum distributions (RMDs) that you must now take from retirement accounts.

5. CHECK WITH THE FEDERAL HOUSING ADMINISTRATION. If your mortgage is insured by the FHA, you might qualify for a so-called streamlined refinance that usually doesn't require an appraisal.

Details: www.hud.gov/offices/hsg/sfh/buying/streamli.cfm and
on the USAgov site at www.FHAgovernmentloans.info.

6. PAY DOWN YOUR PRINCIPAL. If you can add several hundred dollars a month to the principal, lenders will look upon your wish
to refinance more favorably. Or, let your lender know that you
plan to make a lump-sum payment toward your principal. Use
money in a savings account or sell an asset—an extra car, your
80-foot yacht, your coin collection, or investments that have
performed even worse than the rest of the current market and
show no signs of recovery. This would also be a good place for
your tax refund, bonus, or income from moonlighting or a
second job.

7. ADD A NONOCCUPANT COSIGNER TO YOUR LOAN. Not all lenders will
agree to this, but it's worth trying. It's not uncommon with
FHA-insured loans.

!CAUTION A nonoccupant cosigner won't help you overcome bad
credit; it's an option only if your income is not sufficient or
your debt-to-income ratio is too high.

And, if you aren't able to pay back the loan, depending on
your state's laws, the lender can collect from your cosigner
without trying to get the money from you first—including
suing or garnishing your cosigner's wages. If your hope is to
stay lifelong buddies, be very certain that you won't drag your
cosigner into trouble.

8. AGREE TO PAY DOWN DEBTS. If you have enough cash in a savings
account to pay off a credit card debt or a car loan, ask your

lender if doing so will improve your application. Note: This will also help boost your credit score, a major factor in being granted refinancing. (See Chapter 7 for tips on paying down credit card debt.)

9. GET YOUR CREDIT REPORT AND CHALLENGE ANY MISTAKES THAT YOU FIND. Don't be put off by the fact that it takes time to erase errors. Normally, you can deal with such errors within several months. And this, too, boosts your credit score.

10. DRESS NICELY. Appearance counts. You should not walk into a bank asking for a loan (and that's what a refinance is) wearing anything less than "business casual" attire. That's the way the mortgage broker will be dressed. People unconsciously are more inclined to trust those who seem to be like themselves. So no jeans, sweats, or shorts. You want to give the impression that you are serious and reliable and therefore are likely to pay your debts.

REDUCING PROPERTY TAXES

It's easy to be bowled over by an increase in your property taxes. They are often raised during tough times, as localities dealing with budget shortfalls are strapped for money to pay wages and benefits to their teachers, firefighters, police officers, and other employees.

Whether you're facing an increase or simply think that your taxes are too high, there are proven ways to fight back.

The property tax appeal process varies from county to county and from locality to locality. Some places allow home-owners to file their appeal by mail, whereas others require an in-person appearance before a formal appeals board.

How to Appeal

Filing a successful appeal is a detailed and time-consuming process. Read through the steps outlined here and then decide if you want to do it on your own or hire an expert to do the legwork.

STEP 1. Your first step is to find out the deadline for filing an appeal. Simply call your local assessor's office. The deadline typically is 30 to 120 days after assessments are mailed out. This date is important. If you are even one day late, you will have to present your case the following year.

While you have the assessor's office on the phone, ask what the *required appeals procedure* is for your jurisdiction, and ask that copies of any documents explaining the procedure as well as the forms that must be filled out be mailed to you.

Handling Small Mistakes

STEP 2. Next, check your official assessment for common errors. This requires a trip to the assessor's office so that you can read your property record card. You have a legal right to examine this document, which contains all the information that the assessor used to value your property.

Note: The value that an assessor gives a house is based on the market value of the property or a fraction of that value, as determined by law. You'll need to know which system your town uses. If, for example, a house has a market value of $300,000 but the town assesses residential property at 90%, then it is on the books for $270,000. The value is then multiplied by the local tax rate.

Among the mistakes to look for are

- *Typographical errors.* The assessment on the worksheet should match the assessment on your tax bill.
- *Incorrect measurements and descriptions.* Square footage and other dimensions should be accurate. For example, your lot may measure 90 by 200 but could be noted on your card as 190 by 200.
- *Inaccurate numbers.* Review how many bedrooms and bathrooms are listed as well as the total number of rooms. Are you down as having four bedrooms when you really have only three?
- *Age and style.* Is the year your house was built correct? Are you being taxed for a two-story house when you have only one story?

Make a detailed list of any mistakes.

STEP 3. Next, evaluate any important area changes since your last assessment. Certain events decrease a home's value. Note such negatives as a major highway that's been put in near your property, recent encroachment of business zoning, a road expansion, or a widened bridge. Document these with newspaper articles that discuss the change and with photographs. (When photocopying newspaper articles, be sure that the date of the publication is included.)

STEP 4. Ask for an *informal meeting* with the assessor.

Explain the mistakes in a clear, orderly fashion. If you have a recent appraisal of your property that reflects the accurate square footage, the right number of rooms, and other such information, give a copy to the assessor.

In most cases, these fairly simple, obvious errors can be fixed based on your word or after a quick visit to your property by someone from the assessor's office. They rarely require a formal hearing.

After the informal meeting, type up a summary of your findings and mail a copy to the assessor, keeping one for your files. You should receive a corrected assessment within a matter of weeks.

A More Complicated Appeal

If the official documents are correct and/or if you have resolved any small errors informally, the next step in fighting for a lower tax involves evaluating homes similar to yours. This step is based on the fact that you firmly believe that your house will not sell for anywhere near the value given by the city or town's appraiser.

However, to challenge an assessment (beyond the clerical-type errors just covered), you must be able to show that comparable homes in your neighborhood are assessed for less than yours.

STEP 5. Identify comparable properties with lower assessments. Begin by driving around your neighborhood, searching for houses that are like yours in terms of size, style, age, construction, condition, and general location. Jot down the following details for a minimum of three and preferably six comparables. For example:

- *Comparable House 1.* A wood and brick three-bedroom, two-bathroom 1968 Colonial, attached two-car garage, central air conditioning, one fireplace, paved driveway, finished basement, attached deck, small swimming pool, wooded corner lot. Address: 65 Elm Street.

- Then take photos of these comparable houses—visuals not only will make your presentation more professional but will also add credibility to your case.

STEP 6. Return to the assessor's office. Ask for a copy of the property cards for the comparable houses on your list. Add the assessed valuations, square footage, and lot size for each house to your worksheets.

If you find this research project too time-consuming (and it is a very lengthy process) or if you lack the patience to do a thorough job, skip Steps 5 and 6 and jump ahead to Step 7.

STEP 7. Call an area real estate broker. Most brokers (for free, hoping you will list your house with them, or for a small fee) will go through their listings and tell you what comparable houses have sold for and what price yours is likely to bring. Get data, including photos, on three that have sold within the last six months and three that are currently on the market.

If it turns out that the difference between the market value of your home and the assessment is a matter of a few thousand dollars, put the matter to rest. Boards do not want to spend time dealing with small amounts. Your assessor should tell you the circumstances under which appeals are heard. Many will not consider a challenge unless the alleged overassessment is 10% or more.

If the data do not support an appeal, try again next year.

A Formal Hearing

On the other hand, if you decide to move ahead, you will be required to appear before a review board. These boards usually consist of three to five people, either appointed or elected.

At this point, many property owners, if their jurisdiction permits it, decide to hire a licensed appraiser or a property tax attorney to continue with the appeal and represent them. Some of these representatives charge on a contingency basis—that is, they take a percentage of the savings if they are successful in lowering the assessment. Others charge a flat fee or by the hour. Find out before you agree to a deal.

If, on the other hand, you decide to represent yourself, before making an appearance, you need to proceed to Step 8.

STEP 8. Attend several hearings. You are much more likely to win your case if you are familiar with local procedures and the local cast of characters. Sitting in on other grievants' hearings is the best way to learn what works and what does not. Pay attention to the types of presentations given by individual property owners and by competent professionals. How long do they speak? What visuals are effective?

STEP 9. After observing several hearings, file the appropriate papers by certified mail so that you have proof of the date when they were received.

Make enough copies of your case, including pictures and maps, for each member of the review board.

Present your case as professionally as possible. Tempting as it may be, don't rant and rave. Ticking off the appeals board is not the way to win the battle.

In most cases, the board does not make a decision on the spot. Whatever the outcome, the board will pass it on to the assessor. If your town does not inform the grievant by mail, check back with the assessor's office.

> **$ TIP** If your appeal is denied, you may be able to present your case to a state board of review for an impartial opinion. In most states, the assessor is required to give you the appeal form and advise you regarding the exact filing deadline.

THE BOTTOM LINE: If your appeal is unsuccessful, keep in mind that you have the option of returning at the same time next year. And when you do, you'll have a wealth of experience to draw upon.

EXCEPTIONS THAT REDUCE PROPERTY TAXES

Local jurisdictions grant property tax exemptions or refunds for certain categories of individuals. You check with your assessor. Among the most common are

- Blind persons
- Disabled veterans living in special housing
- Low-income people (a.k.a. hardship cases)
- The physically disabled or handicapped
- Senior citizens
- Veterans
- Widows or widowers of veterans

WORDSMARTS

ARM: An adjustable-rate mortgage; it allows the lender to change the interest rate at predetermined intervals. When rates rise, some homeowners find that they can no longer make their monthly payments. Adjustments are typically made at one, three, five, and seven years. The interest rate is based on an index (outside the control of the lending institution), such as U.S. Treasury bills.

DEED IN LIEU OF FORECLOSURE: A procedure that takes place when a home-owner cannot make the mortgage payments and cannot find a buyer, and the lender accepts ownership in place of the amount due on the mortgage.

FORECLOSURE: The legal process through which a home is seized because the owner is behind on mortgage payments and/or property taxes. The property is then sold, and the proceeds are used to pay off the loan and/or the taxes.

FORBEARANCE: A short-term reduction in or suspension of payments.

FOR FURTHER INFORMATION

HOW TO FIGHT PROPERTY TAXES, published by the National Taxpayers Union, is available at many public libraries. To order ($6.95), log on to www.ntu.org or call 703-683-5700.

THE FORECLOSURE SURVIVAL GUIDE, by Attorney Stephen Elias (Berkeley, Calif.: Nolo Publishers, 2008).

7

Surviving Credit Card Crunch

"So far as my coin would stretch;
And where it would not, I have used my credit."
SHAKESPEARE *KING HENRY IV, ACT I, SCENE II*

A small amount of credit card debt is manageable as long as everything is hunky-dory. But if you lose your job, your hours are cut back, you become ill or disabled, or your spouse or partner is unable to work, that debt suddenly looms large. Ditto when you accrue huge medical bills beyond what is covered by your insurance. So read on for reminders on how to avoid serious debt in the first place and what to do if you wind up unable to make your card payments.

PREVENTING SERIOUS CREDIT CARD DEBT

Most Americans, especially those for whom the Great Depression is only a chapter in a history book, have regarded easy credit as their birthright—up until this recession hit with a whammy. And now, many people are waking up each morning to find themselves "another day older and deeper in debt," as Tennessee Ernie Ford crooned in his 1955 hit, "Sixteen Tons." The words of this coal miner's lament (written by Merle Travis) bear repeating:

You load sixteen tons, what do you get?
Another day older and deeper in debt.
Saint Peter, don't you call me, 'cause I can't go;
I owe my soul to the company store.

Whether or not you're a miner, live in Tennessee, or like country-and-western songs, you don't want to wind up owing your soul to your credit card company. It's easy to slip down that path—the expensive dinners, the new car, the Harley, the jewelry and Italian suits, and finally the McMansion will do it.

Credit cards are convenient—there's no argument about that. And in many situations, they're necessary—when booking a hotel room, renting a car, or buying an airline ticket. But you don't need to carry around a pocketful of them, like the famous Mr. Plastic Fantastic (a.k.a. Walter Cavanagh), who has been in the *Guinness Book of World Records* every year since 1971. He holds 1,497 cards. But he uses only one at a time and pays it off in full each month.

TO RECESSION-PROOF
YOUR CREDIT CARD

1. CARRY JUST ONE CARD (UNLESS YOU'RE TRAVELING). Designate in advance what you will use it for: major items (like an air conditioner) that you can afford to pay off quickly, little luxuries such as dinner out once a week, or an online purchase. Otherwise pay cash, write a check, or use a debit card (although see the following discussion of when you might not want to use a debit card).

$ TIP Keep one or two traveler's checks (left over from your last vacation) in your wallet. Use them for an emergency or when you need immediate cash, rather than running up your credit card balance.

2. PLAN OUT-OF-TOWN JOURNEYS IN ADVANCE. When you're traveling, you'll find that some hotels and car rental companies put a temporary charge or lock on your credit card in anticipation of bills. If your limit is low, you may not be able to use your card for any other purpose, so carry a second card just in case. And if you're traveling abroad, find out each of your cards' "conversion fee" for foreign currency transactions (1% to 3% is typical). At least one major card company, Capital One (800-695-5500, www.capitalone.com), does not have such a fee.

3. RUN A TALLY. It's easy to forget what you've charged. Add up your credit card receipts once a week. Is the total within your budget guidelines? If it's not, cut back.

4. GET A CHECKING ACCOUNT WITH AN ATM CARD. Use the card (debit or credit) only for purchases that require a card. But keep a daily record of what you spend so that you don't overdraw your checking account. You can review your balance online or by telephone, but sometimes there is a lag of a day or so before the amount shows up in your electronic records.

$ TIP To be safe, keep a small pad and pencil in your pocket or purse and jot down the figures.

5. PAY CASH. Figure out what your expenses for the week will be, take that amount out of your checking account, and don't go back for more. Personal bonus: If you manage to cut corners and have some left over, keep it in your mayonnaise jar (see Chapter 5 about the benefits of having a personal mayonnaise jar). You might even find that the challenge of cutting corners gets to be fun. And you're allowed to reward yourself with a small splurge from your extra savings.

6. TRACK AUTOMATIC MONTHLY CHARGES. This means those made against your credit card, such as gym membership, Internet services, and regular purchase programs (for vitamins, beauty products, or fruit or flower of the month). They're so easy to forget, and if you're running close, they can send your balance over your credit limit. The subsequent fees for doing so are hefty.

7. READ YOUR STATEMENT CAREFULLY EACH MONTH. Many people opt for electronic statements and payments—an efficient and "green" choice. But don't get complacent and assume that all is well. You might find out months too late that you forgot to cancel that online "free trial" after the "free" part expired. Or worse yet, your payment arrived one day late and you've been hit with the exorbitant "default" rate.

BENEFITS OF PAYING ON TIME

When you get a new credit card, it usually comes with great enticements—maybe 0% on balance transfers and on new purchases. But those goodies don't last forever. In the fine print (which few people bother to read), it might have explained that the deal was for just 12 months, or maybe 18.

The fine print likewise described the official "default rate," also known as the "penalty rate" for a late or missed payment. You may think this will never happen to you, but it's very easy to get caught—you need be only one day late for it to kick in. And if it does, you'll wind up with a late payment fee (routinely $39), and in addition, the credit card company is likely to raise the interest rate on any unpaid balances to 20 to 30%. Worse yet, those high rates could apply to charges you made in the past, if you're carrying an ongoing balance.

And the bad news doesn't stop here. Some credit card companies actually apply the default rate whether or not you've made the payment on their card on time, if they find out you've been late making payments to other lenders, such as your mortgage lender. This is known as a *universal default penalty*.

Meanwhile, if this example doesn't motivate you to pay your credit card bills on time, nothing will. Using Bankrate's minimum payment calculator, let's say that your 0% balance transfer rate has come to an end, and you're now paying 9% on your existing balance of $3,000. If you just pay the minimum ($125 to start), it will take you 191 months (more than 15 years) to be rid of your debt. In that time, you will pay $2,048.71 in interest.

If the rate jumps to 20%, it will take you 369 months (more than 30 years) to be rid of your debt. In that time, you will pay $9,464.79 in interest.

To make certain that you make your payments on time:

- *Arrange for reminders and electronic payments.* Sign up for an e-mail reminder; these typically arrive a week before your payment is due. Most card companies let you set up electronic payments ahead of time so that the money is debited from your account on (or preferably a day or two before) your due date. Some also allow you to arrange for regular monthly payments of the minimum due on your account each month.
- *Know your card company's policy on default rates.* Three of the biggest card issuers, Chase, Citicorp, and Bank of America, do not impose universal default. Check with your issuer, and while you're on the phone, find out exactly what happens if you're even a day late with your payment.
- *Look for options.* If you get caught in a default rate, immediately call the card issuer and complain. You may get a break if you've been a loyal, prompt-paying customer. If the card company won't budge and you have other credit cards, call each of them and ask about balance transfer offers. Or watch the mail for a preapproved offer from another card company.

WHICH CARDS TO PAY OFF FIRST

It seems like a no-brainer—to pay off your higher-rate cards first. To find out how much you'll save by doing so (while continuing to pay the minimum on your other cards) and how long it will take, use Dinkytown's "Credit Card Roll-Down Calculator" at www.dinkytown.com/java/DebtRolldown.html.

The calculator will also tell you how much you'll save on interest if you pay just a little bit more each month on your highest-rate cards. For example, let's say you have balances of $3,000 on an 18.9% card and $4,000 at 17.5%; if you put an additional $25 faithfully toward the highest-interest debt, you'll save $2,416 in interest and roll down your balances to zero in 2 years and 5 months, instead of 11 years and 8 months.

There's another school of thought, however: that you should pay off your lowest balance first, just to give you the boost of erasing one of your balances more quickly. Run the numbers through the calculator to find out how that would affect your savings. For example, if you had a balance of $3,000 on an 18.9% card and $1,000 at 17.5%, and you put that extra $25 toward the lower balance, you'd wind up paying only $8 more in interest to retire that balance first. It might be well worth that small amount to see at least one zero balance a little sooner.

In the end, the goal is to reduce your debt to no more than 10% of your credit line on any single credit card. Like diets, one size doesn't fit all—choose whatever plan you can stick to until the debt is gone.

NEGOTIATING A LOWER INTEREST RATE

It's not automatic, but sometimes it is possible to lower your rate if you're a loyal customer with an excellent payment record (another good reason to meet those due dates). It's a lot more expensive for a card issuing company to find a new customer than to keep you, and more often than not, cardholders are successful in getting a 21% or 18% rate lowered to 15% or 11%.

Here's what you need to know before you make that phone call.

1. TAKE A LOOK AT YOUR CREDIT REPORT. (See the following discussion for details about how to do that.) Make sure you really do have a record of timely payments.

2. PICK A CARD THAT YOU'VE HELD FOR AT LEAST TWO YEARS. You want to be able to make the case that you value the card and want to keep it.

3. BE PERSISTENT BUT POLITE. Mention that you're receiving offers with much better rates from other companies and that you're thinking of moving your business elsewhere. At the same time, mention that you would much rather stay with a card that you know. Ask what's the best rate the bank can offer. If the customer service rep can't help, ask to speak to a supervisor or manager.

TO CONSOLIDATE OR NOT

If you're carrying multiple high-rate balances, you definitely want to move your balances to a card with a low or 0% rate—if you get such a promotional offer. But the savings will be short-term unless you

- Pay as much as you can on the balance during the promotional-rate period (typically 6 to 18 months). It's critical to remember exactly how long that period lasts.
- Stop using that particular card. Your goal is to pay down the balance, not keep it growing.
- Understand the terms. You won't save much if your rate jumps to 21% after 6 months, or to 30% if you miss a payment.

FINDING LOW-INTEREST-RATE CARDS

If you have a good credit rating, you undoubtedly receive offers for cards with a 0% promotional interest rate. Yet as stated earlier, those rates come to an end all too quickly. Before you jump on board, find out where the interest rate is headed once the promotional period is over, especially if you don't anticipate paying off your balance during that time frame. Ideally, you want a rate that's under 10%, but for that you will need great credit.

$ TIP To find credit cards with low interest rates and low or no annual fees, go to www.bankrate.com, www.creditcards.com, and www.lowcards.com. At each site, you can also compare offers and search for such things as reward points, cash back, and special deals.

Wherever you find your new card, use Dinkytown's "Credit Card Payoff Calculator" at dinkytown.com. It will spell out how much you must pay each month if you want to pay off your card during the promotional rate period. Even if you can't manage that amount on a monthly basis, knowing the number will give you an extra incentive to up your payments whenever you can.

USING A HOME EQUITY LOAN

Putting your home on the line to pay off other debts should not be your first choice. Nor should it be a snap decision. It could turn out to be risky, especially in this era of foreclosures.

On the one hand, it can be argued that if you know that you will have no problem making the home equity loan payments, and that you won't rack up additional credit card debt, it's a way to pay off high-rate debts with a low-rate loan—about 5% with a home equity line of credit and 8.5% for a home equity loan (also known as a second mortgage).

To run your personal numbers and see what you would save, use Bankrate's "Debt Consolidation Calculator" at: www. bankrate.com/brm/calculators/loans/debt_consolidation_ calculator.asp.

Even if the results seem overwhelmingly in favor of using a real estate loan to take care of credit card debt, you must be absolutely certain that neither you nor your partner will run up more plastic-related debt. And, you must promise yourself that you will not take out a loan for more than the amount of your credit card debt.

CREDIT VERSUS DEBIT CARDS

When you use a *credit card*, which is a form of revolving credit, you incur debt. (The issuer sets a limit, and you can charge up to that amount. When you make payments, your credit line is replenished by the amount that you pay.)

When you use a *debit card*, you are taking money from your checking or savings account, and that account has already been funded—so you are using your own money. Debit cards do not offer a line of credit.

There are pros and cons to both.

If you pay your balance off in full each month and have a no-annual-fee credit card, you have actually had the use of the money interest-free for a few weeks without dipping into your own cash. Yet it's all too easy to slip into thinking that the line of credit your card offers is already "your" money.

but not the best. A score below 600 (or in some cases below 675) signals high risk to lenders. Your credit score is based on five pieces of information:

1. YOUR PAYMENT HISTORY (35%). This includes how often you have made late payments and whether you've declared bankruptcy. Timely payments help your score; late payments are obviously harmful.

2. HOW MUCH YOU OWE (30%). This includes both balances on all accounts and how many of your accounts actually have balances. It also calculates how much you owe in proportion to how much credit is available to you—in other words, how close you are to your credit limits.

3. THE LENGTH OF YOUR CREDIT HISTORY (15%). Obviously, the longer you have managed credit, the better.

4. HOW MUCH OF YOUR CREDIT IS NEW CREDIT (10%). Applying for new credit temporarily lowers your score by about 5 points.

$ TIP Although FICO scores differentiate between any online searching you do to find the best credit cards and applying for a single mortgage or auto loan, be careful. Do your online credit card search within a single, short period of time so as not to lower your FICO score.

5. TYPES OF CREDIT (10%). This includes how many different kinds of credit you have (credit cards, auto loans, mortgages, business loans, and so on).

You can get your credit score for free from myFICO (www.myFICO.com) as part of a 30-day free trial of the FICO Score Watch. If you don't cancel within 30 days, you're in for an $89.95 annual fee. MyFICO also has several packages that include your score and credit reports from the three agencies for various prices.

A better bet: Get your full credit report (not your score) from Equifax and TransUnion for free once every 12 months from www.annualcreditreport.com, or call 877-322-8228. Having your report in hand makes it possible to boost your score if you spot and correct errors, such as accounts listed as being open long after you've closed them.

To repeat, credit scores are not trivial. They make a huge difference. A person with a score under 600 might pay three percentage points more on a mortgage than someone with a score above 700. (Examples of what rates are offered to people with what scores are spelled out on the myFICO Web site.) And people with good scores receive better credit card offers.

SIX WAYS TO BOOST YOUR FICO SCORE

PAY YOUR BILLS ON TIME. Delinquent payments and collections hurt your score. The longer you pay your bills on time, the better. Calling and explaining why you were late with a payment may help.

KEEP BALANCES ON CREDIT CARDS LOW. High debt levels have a negative impact on your score.

PAY OFF DEBT RATHER THAN MOVING IT BETWEEN CREDIT CARDS. The most effective way to improve your score in this area is to pay down your revolving credit.

APPLY FOR AND OPEN NEW CREDIT ACCOUNTS ONLY WHEN YOU NEED THEM. Too many applications lower your score.

DON'T CLOSE ACCOUNTS WITH UNUSED CREDIT. Your score is based on how high your balance is relative to how much credit is available to you.

CHECK YOUR CREDIT REPORT REGULARLY FOR ACCURACY. Contact the creditor and credit reporting agency to correct any errors.

(Consumer Federation of America and FICO)

THE BOTTOM LINE: Keep the 10% solution in mind. To maintain a high FICO score (720 or more), use no more than 10% of your available balance on any single line of credit.

If your FICO score is not in the good to excellent range, don't panic. Instead, think of it as a snapshot of a single moment, not a sentence of permanent doom. True, late payments, bankruptcies, foreclosures, collections, and the like stay on your credit report for seven years (Chapter 7 bankruptcies for ten years). But even during those seven years, the older the "faux pas" is, the less impact it has. Time heals all.

WORDSMARTS

CHARGE CARD: A card that differs from a credit card in that it doesn't offer a line of credit.

DEFAULT RATE: The interest rate imposed on cardholders who are late in paying their credit card bills or who exceed their credit limit.

FICO: The Fair Isaac Corp., which was founded in 1956 by engineer Bill Fair and mathematician Earl Isaac. It computes credit scores for individuals and sells them to the credit reporting agencies.

PROMOTIONAL RATE PERIOD: The length of time during which a low or zero interest rate (also known as a "teaser" rate) on a credit card is offered.

UNIVERSAL DEFAULT PENALTY: A practice in which a bank increases a cardholder's interest rate because of late payments on "outside" accounts, such as a mortgage, or when the cardholder's FICO score drops. The interest-rate penalty can be imposed even if the cardholder has a flawless payment record on the bank's credit card.

FOR FURTHER INFORMATION

HOW CREDIT SCORING WORKS: www.pueblo.gsa.gov/cic_text/money/creditscores/your.htm.

CREDIT EDUCATION at www.myFICO.com. This Web site has other downloadable brochures on your rights under the Fair Debt Collection Practices Act (FDCPA) as well as calculators to help you figure out what kind of loan you need, how much credit you might have available to you, whether you would benefit by consolidating your debt, and tax savings.

8

Managing Your Brokerage and 401(k) Accounts

"I've been rich and I've been poor. Believe me, honey, rich is better!"

—SOPHIE TUCKER

I want to say up front that it takes a considerable amount of training and experience as well as an inherent sense of the market to become a successful stockbroker or a first-rate money manager. The aim of this chapter is not to turn you into an investment guru overnight. Rather, its intent is to help you work intelligently with your broker and/or to manage your own accounts, so that, like Sophie Tucker, you can be rich, not poor. Sophie, incidentally, started out waiting tables at her parents' Hartford, Connecticut, diner/rooming house and earning tips by singing for customers. When she died in 1966, the famous singer/comedian—also well known for her philanthropy—left a sizable fortune, including an endowed theater arts chair at Brandeis University. May you be able to do the same!

DON'T PANIC

If your accounts have shriveled because of the struggling economy, panic is understandable, but it won't fix anything—however, facing your situation realistically might. If you selected well-run companies, top-rated bonds, and mutual funds with excellent track records, your portfolio or 401(k) account is very likely to recover. Be prepared to be patient, however. Recovery from this recession won't happen overnight. On the other hand, if you have losers, then you're stuck with losers. But even losers have a bright side. Selling them might net you a tax break, as explained later in this chapter.

Before you can monitor your 401(k) or brokerage account intelligently, you need to be clear about two things. The first is why you purchased each investment in the first place. And the second is the difference between *income* and *growth*. If you are investing for income, then you should look to bonds and high-dividend-paying stocks. If you want price appreciation, then growth stocks and growth mutual funds are the answer.

If you confuse income and appreciation, and many people do, you might accidentally sell investments that are growing in value and price because they didn't produce the income for you that you thought they would. On the other hand, you might mistakenly sell income producers because they didn't go up in price. Unless you keep this straight when making investment decisions, it's highly unlikely that you'll make money.

RECESSION-RESISTANT INDUSTRIES

In every phase of the economic cycle, including a recession, there are winners and, of course, losers. Industries that continue to do well, and even thrive, during a down market are those comprising companies that sell products and services that we always need, no matter what's going on in the world. Wall Street refers to these as *recession-resistant industries*. You can identify some, if not all, of these industries on your own. Simply think of the things that people cannot or will not do without. And as you relate this information to your personal portfolio, keep in mind that old adage, "Don't put all your eggs in one basket." Diversify among industries—and then again within each industry you choose.

Beverages. This industry covers both alcoholic and non-alcoholic beverages, including soft drinks. Sales tend to remain strong, even during economic downturns. Some experts maintain that during really tough times, beer sells better than hard liquor because it is less expensive.

Drugs. People continue to buy medicines and over-the-counter drugs. It's difficult, if not plain unwise, to skip your high blood pressure medicine, and it's tough to survive forever without an aspirin or a cough drop.

Food. We will continue to eat. People who are under financial pressure buy bread, milk, soup, pasta, rice, and other staples, but at the same time they look for brands. Gourmet and deluxe lines may not be as profitable. Comfort food, including candy, and inexpensive fast-food chains usually remain winners. Note: The food industry includes production, processing, distribution, stores, and supermarkets.

An interesting bit of trivia: Ritz Crackers were created in 1934 by the National Biscuit Company (now Nabisco) to provide something that was rich-tasting and seemingly luxurious, but still affordable—a box cost 19 cents—to a depression-weary America. Spam, manufactured by Hormel Foods and introduced on July 5, 1937, was a staple for Allied troops overseas during World War II.

Gardening. Seed companies tend to do well as people plant recession gardens. This group includes vegetable seeds and, to a lesser extent, flower seeds, fertilizers, garden tools, and equipment.

Health care and medical supplies. Industries that produce equipment and hospital supplies are essential, especially given our aging population.

Household products. During all economic cycles, we need soap, toothbrushes, and shampoo along with cleaning products for washing clothes, dishes, and floors.

Telephone and telecommunications. Not every company within this group is likely to thrive during an economic setback. Look for players that are well run and carry little debt.

Utilities. There's always a reliable demand for electricity and gas. No one voluntarily signs up to sit in the dark, or to go without heat or air conditioning during temperature extremes. However, utilities with a large component of industrial users might suffer as businesses cut back.

Waste disposal. Garbage collectors and those companies whose activities are mandated by the government, such as hazardous waste disposal, sell services that are needed at all times.

> **$ TIP** Knowing about recession-resistant industries is useful in another way: they are potential places for employment. If you are unemployed or fear that you will be, why not look for a job with recession-resistant companies located in your area?

DIVIDEND-PAYING STOCKS

Another way to invest during hard times is to buy the stocks of companies that have a long history of paying regular dividends. In a poor market, these stocks tend to decline less in price than those that are not dividend-oriented. Why, you might ask? Because institutional and individual investors prize them, hold on to them, and often buy additional shares when prices are down from their previous highs.

Begin by studying Standard & Poor's "S&P 500 Dividend Aristocrats," more than 50 companies that have increased their dividend payout for a minimum of 25 consecutive years. You'll find the list at www.marketattributes.standardandpoors.com. (In the middle of the table, click on "Dividend Aristocrats.") You will recognize many of the names, from Abbott Laboratories and Clorox to McDonald's and Walgreens. These, like many other aristocrats, fall into the recession-resistant stock category mentioned earlier.

DOLLAR COST AVERAGING

One of the most difficult aspects of investing is timing—should you put your money into stocks or mutual funds this week, next week, or months from now? There's a simple formula that gets you around this age-old dilemma—dollar cost averaging.

This involves investing the same amount of money in a stock or mutual fund at fixed intervals—monthly or quarterly, for instance. It may seem dull, but it actually requires personal discipline in down markets, when the overwhelming temptation is not to invest.

Basically, what this technique does is force you to buy more of a stock when the price is low and less when it is high. Over the long haul, your average cost will be lower than the average price of the security.

!CAUTION: Although this is a fine technique, it will not turn a poor investment choice into a winner. Use it with stocks and funds that have a record of long-term upward trends.

CHANGES IN THE DOW

Another investing strategy that is useful during a recession (and one that most investors overlook) involves the Dow Jones Industrial Average—not so much where it is every day, but rather when changes are made in the Dow. In other words, when stocks in the Dow are dropped and replaced by new ones, adding the new companies to your portfolio, while not foolproof, is certainly worth considering.

$ TIP For excellent (and easy-to-understand) information on all the Dow Jones indexes, go to www.djindexes.com.

FOLLOWING THE INSIDERS

This stock-picking strategy involves finding out when executives are buying or selling their own company's stock—something that many Enron employees wish they had known. Transactions by top officers involving company securities must be filed with the SEC on its Form 4. You can track these buy and sell trades using EDGAR (the Electronic Data Gathering, Analysis and Retrieval system) at www.sec.gov/edgar.shtml. The site has a tutorial explaining how to find both up-to-the-minute and historical company filings and even proxy voting records for mutual funds.

The four key forms you should look for are

Form 10-K: Annual audited financial statements

Form 10-Q: Quarterly performance updates

Form 8-K: Key events—mergers, acquisitions, or revised financial data

Insider Trading Forms 3, 4, and 5: Information on trading by company officers and directors

USING VALUE LINE

The *Value Line Investment Survey,* an independently published weekly, follows more than 1,700 stocks within 99 industries. The reports on each industry and the stocks within that industry are revised quarterly. These updates are written by independent securities analysts—in other words, not by analysts working for brokerage firms or investment bankers.

Stocks are ranked (based on proprietary calculations) to predict their probable performance over the next 6 to 12 months—1 to 5 for *timeliness* and 1 to 5 for *safety*.

$ TIP If you were not aware of the importance of company debt prior to this recession, I'm sure you are now. Conservative and semi-conservative investors do not want to invest in companies with high debt levels. The *Value Line Investment Survey* spells out each company's long-term and total debt, invaluable figures for making buy, hold, or sell decisions.

The weekly "Value Line Summary & Index" is extremely useful for making buy, hold, and sell decisions. The Index lists stocks that are ranked 1 or 2 in safety, are regarded as very timely, pay the highest dividends, have the best cash flow, and have the best three- to five-year price potential. You can also run down a list of the last 13 weeks' best- and worst-performing stocks or those with the lowest and highest P/Es. Two additional lists are conservative stocks and bargain basement stocks.

Value Line, which has been in business for more than 75 years, also has free online educational material that is perfect for people who are new to managing their accounts, yet ideal for experienced investors to review. Go to www.valueline.com and click on "Education" to take the tutorial—you'll find out about P/E ratios, target price range, debt levels, and other financial data as well how to use the *Value Line Investment Survey*.

Check to see if your broker or public library subscribes to the *Value Line Investment Survey*. Some libraries, particularly those with healthy budgets, allow patrons to access the library's online subscription from home using their own computers and logging on with their library card ID. You might want to see if your library offers such a service—not just to read the *Value Line Investment Survey*, but as a way to save money on other subscriptions. If your local library does not have such a service, joining a larger library in your area might be worth it, even if you have to pay as an out-of-towner to join.

Or you can subscribe. The online version is $538 per year, or $65 for a 13-week trial. Multiuser subscriptions are available by calling 800-531-1425. The print subscription is $598 per year or $75 for a 13-week trial; call 800-833-0046.

USING THE *OUTLOOK*

For over 85 years, Standard & Poor's has published the popular weekly *Outlook*, which has research on individual stocks, special reports on the economy, and articles on personal finance topics. Particularly useful for anyone monitoring a portfolio are the "Strong Buy" or five-star stock recommendations. The online edition (www.spoutlook.com) is $199 per year or $19.50 per month. The print version, which includes access to online features, is $298 per year, with 20 percent off for new subscribers; call 800-852-1641.

KNOWING WHEN TO SELL

Financial whiz kids and Wall Street gurus are always weaving complex theories about when to buy a stock. That's the easy part. However, they shy away from explaining when to sell, which is a much trickier business.

Although there's no foolproof system for making certain that you always buy low and sell high, you can make educated decisions.

1. The first basic rule to follow in mastering the art of selling is to know whether you purchased a stock or mutual fund for growth or income—as mentioned at the beginning of this chapter.

2. The second rule is to set target prices. When you buy shares in a mutual fund or company, write down a target price. When your investment reaches that price, sell it. If you have a strong sense that the investment will continue to grow in value, sell one-third or one-half of your position.

3. Third, seriously consider selling if you think (or definitely know) that the company is in trouble, its earnings prospects are poor, and it's unlikely to recover quickly. As Warren Buffett, chairman of Berkshire Hathaway, Inc., and a true Wall Street guru, has said: "Should you find yourself in a chronically leaking boat, energy devoted to changing vessels is likely to be more productive than energy devoted to patching leaks."

4. Fourth, if your stock or mutual fund suddenly drops in price by 20% or more within a short time period (a month or less), you need to find out why and then, based on the facts, consider selling.

5. Fifth, if you would not buy the stock at its current price, then sell. (If the company recovers and the price starts to rise, you can always slowly repurchase shares.)

Here is one way to protect your position on the downside and another to protect your profits on the upswing:

- *Enter stop-loss orders.* Tell your broker to sell your stock if it drops to a specific price. This protects you from losing more than a specific amount and, to some extent, against major declines.

- *Sell into strength.* Each time the market makes a major move on the upside, sell a portion of your holdings. For example, if you own 500 shares of Company XYZ and you have big gains, sell 100 shares each time it appreciates by 10%. You reduce your risk, and at the same time you're selling your stock at higher prices.

Finally, review the holdings in your 401(k) account and your brokerage portfolio on a regular basis. Don't go crazy and look at them every day, but do check in at least quarterly or monthly. Look to see if any of your holdings have reached their target prices or if any have dropped significantly in price. Then make your educated decision.

Note: Don't fall in love with your investments. If you do, you will never sell and take your profits. And you will never sell to cut your losses.

BEING WORTHLESS

We mentioned earlier that it's almost impossible not to own some losers during a recession (or, actually, during any segment of the economic cycle). The only good news, and it's semi-good, is that if you own a stock that is officially worthless, you may get a tax break. However, just because a company is in bankruptcy doesn't mean that its stock is worthless in the eyes of the ever-watchful IRS.

In order to be eligible for the so-called worthless stock break, the stock must meet two qualifications. One, it can no longer be trading on any of the exchanges, over the counter, or through the pink sheets. Two, it must have absolutely zero value. It cannot be worth even one cent—if it is, the IRS, naturally, maintains that it has value.

However, proving worthlessness is very difficult. Sometimes a stock can be purchased after delisting as well as right after bankruptcy. You should check with your broker or accountant.

Investors are allowed to treat a stock that has no value as if it is a capital asset that was sold for zero on the last business day of the year.

Although investors are not required to spell out the details on their tax return, I strongly recommend that you save all documentation relating to the stock's loss of value. That includes notices that you received from the company, news articles (with the date showing) about the situation, and anything else that appears relevant. It is particularly important to have proof of the date the stock became worthless, in case you are audited. If you don't know the date, call the company's headquarters and ask for Investor Relations. Even though the firm is in bankruptcy, there is probably a skeleton staff on hand. A broker will also know the date.

Then report the worthless stock on IRS Schedule D and attach it to your 1040.

SELLING AT A LOSS

Losses are hard to take, but if they are not in your retirement account, they may reduce your taxes.

If your stock turns out not to be officially worthless and is still trading, but at pathetically low prices, you can opt to sell your shares at a loss and use this loss to offset any capital gains you made during the year. This can be done on a dollar-for-dollar basis up to $3,000 per year ($1,500 for married filing separately) for as long as it takes to use up the loss.

Note: If you had more capital losses than gains (which we hope was not the case), then your losses can be used to offset, dollar-for-dollar, all of your investment gains up to the amount of the loss. If you still have leftover losses, you can offset up to $3,000 of ordinary income each year until the amount of the loss is used up. (Ordinary income is income other than capital gains; it includes wages; salary; any interest earned from savings accounts, bank CDs, and other such assets; dividend payments; and net income from a business.)

If you still have questions about the procedure, read the section on capital losses in IRS Publication 550, "Investment Income & Expenses," available at www.irs.gov. (This is a useful guide for all investors to have on hand.)

HOW NOT TO BE MADOFFED

Some say that it's the largest Ponzi scheme in American history. Others are hedging a bit and saying that it's one of the largest. Either way, it's been disastrous for those who invested with Bernard L. Madoff Investment Securities. The list is long and includes charities, individual investors, and people in the news. Madoff's Ponzi scheme managed to fool a great many very smart and very prominent Americans.

A Ponzi scheme is based on the "let's rob Peter to pay Paul" principle. In other words, as new money comes in from investors, that money is used to pay off earlier investors. The success of the scheme lies in recruiting new investors. Fraudsters who are selling the promise of sky-high returns in a short time period typically encourage individual participants to bring in their friends.

At some point, the scheme simply gets too big and the promoter is unable to raise enough money from new investors to pay previous investors. The pyramid collapses, and many people, especially those who came into the game late, lose money. That's clearly what happened with those who trusted Madoff.

Eight Ways to Avoid Being Madoffed

1. DIVERSIFY. The first lesson is one you've heard before: diversify. Granted, any money you might have placed in Mr. Madoff's hands (or in the hands of any con artist) would have been lost, but if you didn't put all your money with him, at least you would still have a non-Madoff nest egg.

2. DO IN-DEPTH RESEARCH. You would if you were looking for a doctor. Find out as much as you can about the broker, financial advisor, or hedge fund manager you are considering. Most people choose such an advisor based on personal referral, and referrals are a good place to begin. But again, look at what happened to the people whose friends and colleagues referred them to Madoff.

In addition to using referrals, insist on meeting the advisor or broker in person. If he is too busy, forget about it. If he seems too smooth, forget about it. If he talks down to you, uses a lot of fancy jargon, or spins stories, forget about it.

Ask tough questions about the advisor's performance—and don't believe in unusually high returns. You know what the market is doing, how mutual funds are performing, where the Dow and the S&P 500 are, and what interest rate banks and credit unions are paying on CDs. So, if someone in a suit promises you triple those amounts, you should see a very large red flag.

A good advisor should never promise you a specific return—returns are unknown except in the case of interest-bearing investments.

When you ask what research, strategies, or techniques the advisor uses, look for clear answers. Walk away if you're told, "It's proprietary." All secret schemes are to be avoided. Instead, the advisor should discuss whether you'll be investing in a growth product, an income product, a balanced portfolio, or an arbitrage situation. Or perhaps the investment selection process is based on technical analysis. You don't need to understand every nuance of the firm's strategy, but whoever is running the show should be willing to explain it clearly and in general terms. Also, the results for the previous one to five years should be spelled out in writing.

If you feel positive about the person you are interviewing, conclude by asking for the names of current and former clients. Then call and talk to each one. Ask their opinions. Listen carefully.

3. CHECK A FIRM'S REGISTRATION. As part of your research, take the time to make certain that the firm you do business with or may do business with is registered. Generally, a firm that manages less than $25 million must register with the state or states in which it conducts business or has clients. Firms that manage more than $30 million in client assets must register with the SEC. Firms that manage between $25 and $30 million can choose whether to register with applicable states or with the SEC.

$ TIP To find your state's contact information, go to the North American Securities Association's Web site at www.nasaa.org.

Form ADV comes in two sections. Part I discloses information about the advisory company's business—who owns or controls the company, and whether the company or any of its personnel have had disciplinary sanctions for violating securities or other laws. Part I is filed electronically with the SEC at www.adviserinfo.sec.gov/IAPD/Content/IapdMain/iapd_SiteMap.aspx.

Part II has information on a company's services, fees, and investment strategies. The SEC does not require firms to file Part II electronically, but they are required to deliver Part II or an equivalent document with the same information to all clients before the client signs a contract with them.

$ TIP When you do an actual search, go down to item 11 on ADV Part I(A), "Disclosure Information." Here you will find out what kind of fines or disciplinary action has been taken against the firm. Then at least you can query the broker and do some research on the infraction. Many brokers have infractions, some of them seemingly minor. Ask your accountant to help you evaluate the information if you find it confusing.

! CAUTION Before you invest with a company, make sure that it gives you Part II of its Form ADV. Never do business with a firm (or an advisor) who does not willingly hand over this form.

4. RUN A CHECK ON YOUR BROKER. Information about a registered representative, more commonly known as a stockbroker or account executive, can be found on the Financial Industry Regulator Authority's Web site at www.finra.org. In the "Investors" section, you'll find FINRA's BrokerCheck. Enter the individual broker's name to learn

- Whether the broker is currently suspended or inactive with any regulator
- The types of exams the broker has passed
- The broker's employment history for the past 10 years, including nonsecurities industry employment
- Whether there are any customer disputes, disciplinary actions, or regulatory events that have been reported to the regulatory agencies (along with other financial disclosures, such as bankruptcies filed less than 10 years ago and unpaid judgments or liens)

5. KNOW WHERE YOUR MONEY IS. Your assets should be with a third-party custodian. That means that when you make deposits into your account, you should never be asked to write a check made out to an advisory firm or an individual. The check should be made out to the name of a broker-dealer or mutual fund firm or insurance firm—whichever is the custodian of the money being invested.

6. FIND OUT HOW LIQUID YOUR ACCOUNT WILL BE. This should be in writing. You want quick access to your money. As explained earlier, a pyramid scheme depends upon investors staying with the program and not pulling out.

Hedge funds, for example, often require investors to remain invested for a minimum period of time. Some also limit withdrawals to certain dates, say quarterly. Others insist on 30 days' notice. A lack of liquidity, which was the case with Madoff, is a warning sign. By comparison, think how quickly you can get your money out of the standard mutual fund—one day after you put in your sell order.

7. READ YOUR MONTHLY STATEMENTS. Each one should specify the names of the securities held in the account, the number of shares of each, and the account's value. If you have any doubts about the truthfulness of a statement, ask your accountant to read it with you.

!CAUTION Find out how long it is between the reporting period and when you physically receive an account of activity. The longer this period is, the more worrisome. Let's say you should receive monthly statements, but they actually arrive two months later. That's too long after the fact to make intelligent decisions, such as whether to stay put or to liquidate all or part of your account. It could be a sign that the advisor is doing what Madoff did—sending out fraudulent statements.

You want to do business with a firm or a personal advisor who sends out brokerage statements from a third-party clearinghouse (a company that services financial transactions) that is not affiliated with the firm. It's also a good sign (but not required) if you can get real-time account information via the Internet.

Keep in mind that the Madoff firm was, first of all, the investment advisor. Yet the firm was also the broker, the clearing agent, and the custodian for all the accounts, as well as the firm sending out all customer statements. Lots of red flags there.

THE BOTTOM LINE: There should never be a relationship between the investment advisor and those who provide the clearing services and the custody of the firm's accounts.

8. GO WITH SIPC. Invest only with a brokerage firm that has insurance provided by the Securities Investor Protection Corporation, known as SIPC. The organization's Web site explains why:

> *SIPC is the U.S. investor's first line of defense in the event a brokerage firm fails, owing customer cash and securities that are missing from customer accounts. SIPC either acts as trustee or works with an independent court-appointed trustee in a brokerage insolvency case to recover funds. . . . Funds from the SIPC reserve are available to satisfy claims of each customer up to a maximum of $500,000.*

This figure includes a maximum of $100,000 on claims for cash.

$ TIP Download "The Investor's Guide to Brokerage Firm Liquidations: What You Need to Know & Do" at www.SIPC.org.

┌─ **WORDSMARTS** ─┐

ADV FORM: Documentation required by the SEC from a professional investment advisory firm that spells out the firm's investment style, the amount of assets under management, and the identity of key officers of the firm. The form must be updated annually and be made available as a public record for companies managing in excess of $25 million.

BROKER-DEALER: A firm that operates both as a broker (by bringing buyers and sellers together) and as a dealer (by taking positions of its own in certain securities). Many firms that the public and press call brokerage firms are in fact broker-dealers.

CLEARINGHOUSE: A financial services company that acts as an intermediary for financial transactions.

CUSTODIAN: A bank, trust company, or other organization that is responsible for safeguarding financial assets.

DOW JONES INDUSTRIAL AVERAGE: A measure of market movement based on the stock price movements of 30 leading U.S. corporations.

FINANCIAL ANALYST: A person who studies companies and industries in order to make buy and sell recommendations. Most analysts work for brokerage firms, bank trust departments, or mutual fund companies.

HEDGE FUND: A private investment company whose managers are allowed to use techniques that are generally prohibited in other types of funds. These strategies, including selling short, are generally high in risk. Investments in most hedge funds are available only to professionals and wealthy investors.

NASDAQ: A computerized stock exchange that has no physical presence. It is home to thousands of actively traded over-the-counter stocks, including many high-tech companies. Created in 1971, the Nasdaq was the first electronic stock market and its name was an acronym for National Association of Securities Dealers Automated Quotation. Today it is just Nasdaq.

P/E RATIO: A measure calculated by dividing the current price of the stock by the company's annual earnings per common share over the past 12 months. Example: if the current price of a stock is $50 and its earnings are $5.00 a share, its P/E is 10. This ratio expresses how much investors are willing to pay for the company's earnings. A high P/E may indicate either that there is high expectation that the company will perform well or that it is overpriced. A low P/E might mean the market has lost its confidence in the company or that it's a good time to buy before the P/E rises.

PINK SHEETS: The daily listing of price quotations of over-the-counter stocks. Unlike companies that trade on a stock exchange, companies quoted on the pink sheets are not required to meet minimum requirements or file with the SEC. Before the electronic era, the prices were actually printed on pink paper.

REGISTERED REPRESENTATIVE: A person who works for a brokerage company who is licensed by the Securities and Exchange Commission (SEC) and acts as an account executive for clients for whom she can trade stocks, bonds, and mutual funds. Also known as an account executive. Registered reps (as they are commonly called) must pass the Series 7 and Series 63 securities examinations.

STANDARD & POOR'S 500 STOCK INDEX: Also known as the S&P 500. Compiled by Standard & Poor's company, it includes 500 of the leading and largest companies in the stock market. Because the Dow contains only 30 stocks, many regard the S&P 500 as "the" market.

TECHNICAL ANALYSIS: An investment technique using charts and computer analysis programs (rather than earnings and cash flow) to isolate stock price and volume movements.

FOR FURTHER INFORMATION

HOW THE STOCK MARKET WORKS, 3rd ed., by John M. Dalton (Upper Saddle River, N.J.: Prentice Hall, 2006.)

SECURITY ANALYSIS, 6th ed., by Benjamin Graham and David L. Dodd (New York, N.Y.: McGraw-Hill, 2008).

SOUND INVESTING, by Kate Mooney and Kerry Marrer (New York, N.Y.: McGraw-Hill, 2008).

9

Saving and Paying for College

"A lot of fellows nowadays have a B.A., M.D., or Ph.D.
Unfortunately they don't have a J.O.B."
—"FATS" DOMINO

When the economy is less than robust, it's difficult to set aside tuition money—paying the mortgage, keeping your car on the road, putting food on the table, and buying the kids clothes logically take precedence.

Yet you should not be discouraged. No matter how old your children are and no matter what your financial circumstances are, there are steps you can take to keep college in their future. And schools are working hard to make it possible. In fact, if your child is accepted at Harvard and your total income is less than $60,000, he can attend for free. If your total income is between $60,000 and $180,000, you will pay Harvard approximately 10% of your income. (Your student, however, must contribute a total of $4,000 by working during the school year and/or summer, or through loans.) Yale and many other schools have similar plans.

The government, too, is lending a helping hand via the 2009 stimulus package. Parents of dependent college students can claim a tax credit of up to $2,500 a year to offset the cost of tuition, textbooks, other course materials, and fees. Single filers with adjusted gross incomes of up to $80,000 can claim the full credit. Married couples with an adjusted gross income of up to $160,000 can claim the full amount. Keep in mind, too, that according to the College Board, more than $143 billion in financial aid is available to students for 2009. Here's how you can get some of it to come your way.

COLLEGE BOUND

The College Board estimates that having a bachelor's degree means 60% more in earnings (more than $800,000 during a lifetime) than just having a high school diploma. But if for various reasons your child doesn't attend college, you should not despair. Instead, encourage her strengths, talents, skills, and enthusiasms, keeping in mind that a number of successful Americans did not graduate from college. Yet they all had one thing in common— they were hardworking. Among them: William Faulkner, Bill Gates, Steve Jobs, Mary Pickford, Harry Truman, Mark Twain, George Washington, Woodrow Wilson, and Anna Wintour.

Will Rogers, one of Hollywood's greatest actors (and during the 1930s, the highest paid), left school in the tenth grade. He admitted that he wasn't a good student and "studied the Fourth Reader for 10 years." So college, although it is advisable for many, is not the solution for all.

THE HIGH SCHOOL YEARS

The most worrisome time for parents is when their children are within two years of graduating from high school. While they are in onesies, training bras, and short pants, the pressure is not nearly so intense. So let's start with high school.

As a parent, you will be most successful if you are armed with information, keep key dates in mind, and are well organized. Waiting to do things at the last minute in this particular parental role is courting disaster.

The First Four Steps

First, you should begin the *get-to-know-thy-guidance-counselor effort* by the end of your child's freshman year or the beginning of sophomore year. Knowing this person will make it easier to call or e-mail her to find out about financial aid workshops run by the school, details on local scholarships, plus advice on the college application process. Your child's school most likely maintains bulletin boards posted with information about such things as upcoming college fairs and visits from college recruiters. Make a point of checking these often—and getting your guidance counselor's input if there's something that interests your child.

Second, order a free copy of "Funding Education beyond High School: The Guide to Federal Student Aid," which is available in English and Spanish at school financial aid offices, online at http://studentaid.ed.gov (click on "Tools & Resources," then choose "Publications"), or by calling 800-433-3243.

Third, spend some some time going over the general information provided by the College Board. Your first read should be the section for parents at www.collegeboard.com/parents/ pay. It explains everything from how to apply for scholarships and other aid to understanding the award letter you'll get from any school to which your child has applied for financial assistance.

Fourth and finally, move on to Sallie Mae (http://go. salliemae.com/plan) for a clear overview of the loans for which both students and parents can apply. The site also has a calculator that estimates how much each school would cost you for four years, and what your options might be for loans to fill in any gaps—after you've factored in what you can afford to pay and any scholarships and grants that your student has been awarded.

Loans versus Grants

Before going any further, you want to keep straight in your mind the difference among loans, grants, and scholarships. A loan is money that you must pay back, usually with interest. Loans may be private or from the government. Neither grants nor scholarships need to be paid back. The difference: a scholarship is given in recognition of achievement, while a grant is just given outright.

The best type of loan is one that's subsidized by the federal government. The two major players in this field are *Stafford loans* and *Perkins loans*. Stafford loans can be either subsidized or unsubsidized. Subsidized loans are awarded based on financial need [you must fill out a Free Application for Federal Student Aid, or FAFSA (discussed later in this chapter) to determine need status], and the government pays the interest on them until the student starts repayment after graduation. Unsubsidized Stafford loans are not based on need—any student can apply for one. The interest starts as soon as the loan is disbursed to the school and continues until the loan is paid in full.

As we go to press, with a Stafford loan, dependent students can borrow up to $5,500 ($3,500 subsidized, $2,000 unsubsidized) a year in the freshman year, $6,500 ($4,500 subsidized, $2,000 unsubsidized) in the sophomore year, and $7,500 ($5,500 subsidized, $2,000 unsubsidized) in the junior and senior years—at 6%. Students are approved for a loan based on financial need, and the loan is made through a private lender. Once your FAFSA is processed (see the following discussion), your school will send you a letter apprising you of your loan eligibility, and your school's financial aid office will assist you with the application.

With the federal Perkins loan, the maximum is $4,000 per undergraduate year with a fixed 5% interest rate. These are school-awarded, based on need according to a standard calculation that is applied to information submitted on your FAFSA. They are taken out in the student's name. Approximately 1,800 postsecondary institutions participate in the Perkins loan program. If your school is a participant, the school will determine if you qualify.

Even better than loans are *federal grants* (which never need to be repaid) and *federal work-study awards*, in which students get paid to work at campus jobs, for instance in the dining hall or library.

$ TIP The U.S. Department of Education has details on these programs, along with chapter and verse on federal loans, at http:// studentaid.ed.gov.

The Dreaded FAFSA

When you apply to a college, you generally must fill out a FAFSA (Free Application for Federal Student Aid), whether you will need aid or not. The application is sent in during your child's senior year of high school, with a renewal each year that he is in college. You can get the application from your high school guidance counselor or online at www.fafsa.ed.gov.

All college applications have a place to check if you will need financial aid. Once your child has been accepted by the school, if you indicated that you need aid, the college financial aid office will send you details regarding what you qualify for—work-study, subsidized and unsubsidized loans, Perkins loans, grants, scholarships, and so on. For example, if, based on the FAFSA, it is determined that you can afford to spend $10,000 a year on college costs, the school gives you a package of loans, grants, scholarships, and work-study that covers the rest. If you then get another scholarship or grant (money that doesn't have to be paid back) for, say, $5,000, the school will adjust its package to be $5,000 less.

Filling out the FAFSA is almost as difficult as graduating with honors. Have on hand your income tax return, your student's income tax return, your W-2s and other wage information for the prior year, current bank account statements, and investment income statements.

The form cannot be filed until January 1. Keep in mind that some schools have very early application deadlines, in January even. Check the dates carefully. The FAFSA allows you to do an estimated calculation if you haven't done your taxes.

$ TIP Well-informed counselors at Federal Student Aid Information Center, 800-4-FED-AID, and on the FAFSA Web site will answer your questions. Also check the FAQ on the FAFSA site.

Don't overlook *local scholarships.* Your child's guidance counselor can also direct you toward these, which come in all kinds, shapes, and sizes. Check local organizations and ethnic groups—such as Italian, Greek, Russian, or Polish social clubs, if that is your background. Those who can trace their roots back to early English settlers should look for money provided by the Daughters of the American Revolution.

And then there are local businesses and organizations. Some high schools administer all or most local scholarships through a committee. You fill out one application, then the committee culls what's available and matches the applicants with the ones that are most appropriate.

$ TIP For other scholarships, search online using "scholarships for college," "scholarships for women," or other such qualifiers.

WHEN FINANCIAL AID ISN'T ENOUGH

Once you've found out what your child is being offered in financial aid from scholarships, grants, work-study, and subsidized loans, you'll know how much of a financial shortfall, if any, you're facing. You have several options, the first of which doesn't even require you to take out a loan.

Tuition Payment Plans

Before you take out a loan, look at how much you can afford to pay on a monthly basis toward your child's college bill. A number of services offer parents interest-free monthly payment plans for a low annual fee ($25 to $60). These plans can often be custom-tailored so that multiple individuals (say, two divorced parents or a parent and grandparent) can each make payments on their own. Plan administrators will also help you combine a tuition payment plan with a low-cost loan to reduce the amount you'll have to borrow and thus significantly lower your future interest payments.

$ TIP The college financial aid office will tell you which service the school works with. Meanwhile, gather more details on the FinAid site at www.finaid.org/otheraid/tuition.phtml.

In the "Ask the Aid Advisor" section, you can e-mail your financial aid questions, and you will receive a response from one of more than 100 financial aid advisors who volunteer their time.

Unsubsidized Stafford Loans

To make up a shortfall, students can apply for an unsubsidized $2,000 Stafford loan. Unlike the subsidized version, the interest (currently 6%) keeps accruing during college. But it's still a good deal, since the interest rate is relatively low and repayment doesn't start until six months after leaving school. (Be sure to fill out the FAFSA; you have to be evaluated for the subsidized Stafford loan before you can be granted the unsubsidized version. But the unsubsidized loan is not based on the student's financial need or on creditworthiness.)

PLUS Loans

With the federal *PLUS* (Parent Loans for Undergraduate Students) program, you can borrow up to the total cost of attendance without demonstrating financial need. PLUS loans are not subsidized, and you can choose one of three repayment plans. Your credit history will be checked, but it's a less rigorous evaluation than for a mortgage. The lender will be looking for late payments (90 days or more), bankruptcy, and foreclosure. The rate is currently 8.5% fixed with a 3% origination fee.

$ TIP You may get a 0.25% break on the interest if you set up the repayments to come directly out of your bank account. You can apply online at www.parentplusloan.com or through your bank.

Private Loans

If your FICO score falls into the very good category, you will probably qualify for a private loan from a bank, credit union, or other financial institution.

Home Equity Loans

When the real estate market was robust, these loans were popular with parents of college-bound students. However, even though the interest is tax-deductible, with home values tumbling and foreclosures rising, they are no longer an automatically smart choice.

Keep in mind that a PLUS loan is fully insured against death and disability and that payments can be deferred if you are having financial difficulties. This is not likely with a home equity loan. And few parents have enough equity in their homes to cover all four years for all of their children.

Retirement Accounts

This is another potential source of college funds, but one that comes with major pitfalls. Whether you tap into a 401(k) or an IRA, you are probably taking money out of an account that has already been hard hit by the economic downturn. Second, if you take a loan from your 401(k), you will be borrowing pretax dollars and paying them back with after-tax funds. Finally, if you lose your job, you may be required to repay a 401(k) loan within 30 to 90 days of your last day of work.

With an IRA, you can avoid a 10% early withdrawal penalty if you use the money for college expenses, but you'll still have to pay taxes on the amount you withdraw. (See Chapter 4 for more details on loans and early withdrawals from retirement accounts.)

$ TIP If, despite my caveats, you're considering tapping your retirement accounts to pay for tuition, first read the College Board's advice at www.collegeboard.com/parents/pay/loan-center/ 37050. html.

A PLUS VERSUS
A PRIVATE LOAN

Simple Tuition (www.simpletuition.com) is *the* place to compare financing options for education expenses. For example, if you have a good FICO score (760 or above), a $10,000 private loan would cost less than a PLUS.

The private loan that Simple Tuition found had a rate of 2.72%, with no fees and a 2% "graduation reward" (a 2% rebate on the outstanding principal of the loan after the student graduates—which would amount to $200 if you have deferred repayment until graduation).

The payments would be as low as $73.62 a month, have a term of 15 years, and cost a total of $13,250.97.

However, if your FICO score isn't in the top category, the interest rate could be as high as 7.72%, in which case that same loan would cost a total of $21,444.80!

Note: If you're uncomfortable taking a chance on variable rates (or if you don't qualify for the lowest interest rate and other preferred items like no fees), the PLUS loan would probably be a better choice.

Other factors to consider when comparing these two loans:

- The interest on PLUS loans is tax-deductible for people with incomes under $70,000 (single) or $140,000 (joint).

- The interest on a private loan is not tax-deductible.

- PLUS loans are insured against death and disability of parents and students.

- With PLUS loans, parents are on the hook for the total amount of the loan.

- With a private loan (which is usually cosigned with your student or in the student's name with the parent as cosigner), your name can be removed as a cosigner after 36 to 48 months of prompt payments.

WHAT YOUR STUDENT CAN DO

Children can directly help reduce their college costs and the need for loans. Discuss with them the fact that they could or should

1. DO WELL ACADEMICALLY. Colleges (both public and private) offer substantial tuition grants to top students to ease the financial bite. In most cases, the student needs excellent grades for all four years, although the last two are usually weighted more heavily. In other words, getting As for three years and then slacking off during your senior year will look worse than if you had to struggle during freshman year and were making top grades the rest of high school.

2. TAKE COLLEGE-LEVEL COURSES IN HIGH SCHOOL. Advanced Placement courses are widely accepted for credit by colleges. Less frequently accepted, although worth checking into, are courses taken at community colleges. You'll save on tuition costs and possibly graduate early, saving on room and board.

3. BE AN OUTSTANDING ATHLETE. Schools court high school athletes and grant scholarships to stars in hopes of pumping up their own teams.

4. SAVE THEIR OWN MONEY. When children receive cash from their aunts and uncles and anyone else, have them set aside half the amount in their "college account." And work out a plan so that a percentage of the money they earn from weekend and summer jobs also goes into their college account.

> **$ TIP** Don't put too much money in your child's name, even though it's usually taxed at a lower rate than yours. Colleges use a financial aid formula that assesses a family's need based on up to 5.64% of the parents' available assets and 20% of the assets in a child's name or in a custodial account.

5. LIVE AT HOME AND GO TO COMMUNITY COLLEGE FOR TWO YEARS. Then transfer to a four-year institution. Remind your student that the name of the college she graduates from is the one that goes on the résumé.

6. TAKE SUMMER CLASSES WHILE IN COLLEGE. Again, you might wind up shaving a semester or more off your tenure at college. Just be absolutely sure that your credits will be accepted by your college if you take the classes elsewhere.

7. JOIN AMERICORPS VISTA FOR A YEAR. Participants receive a modest living allowance, health benefits, and either a $4,725 Segal AmeriCorps Education Award toward tuition or $1,200 after completing the program. Details: www.americorps.org.

8. SIGN ON FOR THE TEACHER EDUCATION ASSISTANCE FOR COLLEGE & HIGHER EDUCATION GRANT PROGRAM. TEACH offers up to $4,000 per year to students who agree to teach in "high-need" fields (such as science, math, and special education) in schools that serve students from low-income families. Details: http://student aid.ed.gov/PORTALSWebApp/students/english/TEACH.jsp, or call 800-4-FED-AID.

9. LOOK INTO OTHER HIGH-DEMAND CAREERS. In some cases, federal student loans are forgiven for those who become nurses, medical technicians, or law enforcement officers. Details: http://student aid.ed.gov/students/attachments/funding/ StudentGuide0809_ RepayingLoan.pdf.

10. CHECK OUT THE BENEFITS OF ROTC (AND COMMITTING TO MILITARY SERVICE AFTER COLLEGE) OR GOING TO COLLEGE ON THE NEW GI BILL AFTER MILITARY SERVICE. Details: www.military.com and www.vba.va.gov.

The new Post 9/11 GI Bill consists of education assistance programs run by the Department of Veterans Affairs to benefit veterans, service members, and some dependents of disabled or deceased veterans. Under the new benefits, which go into effect August 1, 2009, many veterans who served after 9/11 get full college tuition and fees, as well as $1,000 per year for books and supplies.

Note: Members of the Reserve and National Guard who have been activated for more than 90 days since 9/11 receive the same benefits.

ROTC (Reserve Officers' Training Corps) allows you to take a regular college curriculum plus certain specialized courses while training to become an officer in the Air Force, Army, or Navy upon graduation. In addition to having your tuition partially or completely paid by the government, you can get a non-taxable monthly allowance ($250 to $400 for Air Force ROTC) and travel free on space-available military flights.

14 TUITION-FREE COLLEGES

These schools do not charge tuition. In some instances, students must agree to work on campus or serve in the military.

COLLEGE	LOCATION
Alice Lloyd College	Pippa Passes, Kentucky
Berea College	Berea, Kentucky
City University of New York Teacher's Academy	New York, New York
College of the Ozarks	Point Lookout, Missouri
Cooper Union	New York, New York
Curtis Institute of Music	Philadelphia, Pennsylvania
Deep Springs College	Deep Springs, California
F. W. Olin College	Needham, Massachusetts
U.S. Air Force Academy	Colorado Springs, Colorado
U.S. Coast Guard Academy	New London, Connecticut
U.S. Merchant Marine Academy	Kings Point, New York
U.S. Military Academy	West Point, New York
U.S. Naval Academy	Annapolis, Maryland
Webb Institute	Glen Cove, New York

WHAT PARENTS CAN DO

When you followed the first four steps in this chapter—as I know you religiously did— you read the information about various financial aid plans. There's no need to repeat that information, but I do want to give you a few more bits of advice.

The earlier you start, the better. Even a small amount saved regularly can pack a punch provided you start early enough, like when your baby is still in a bassinette. Investing just $100 a month for 18 years will create $48,000, assuming an 8% average annual return.

Take advantage of state-sponsored 529 savings plans. They come in two varieties—prepaid tuition and savings. They also vary widely from state to state, but they typically have a number of pluses: qualified withdrawals are free of federal tax and sometimes have state tax breaks as well, and many state plans allow you to save more than $300,000 per beneficiary (the amount varies by state). You also have the flexibility of changing the beneficiary without penalty. Details: www.savingforcollege.com.

$ TIP The Hope Credit and Lifetime Learning Credit also come with tax breaks. *Details:* IRS Publication 970, "Tax Benefits for Education," at www.irs.gov.

Arrange your financial life to maximize your eligibility for financial aid. Among the best strategies:

- *Save money in your name.* Not the student's.
- *Spend down your student's assets and income.* Then turn to yours.
- *Clean up debt.* Pay off credit cards and car loans to boost your eligibility for PLUS and other loans.
- *Maximize contributions to your retirement account.* Retirement funds are sheltered from need basis calculations.
- *Reduce your available cash.* If you need to make a large necessary purchase, do it during the base year—January through December of the year before your child will start college, which is the year used to determine eligibility for financial aid.
- *Sell bad investments.* And incur a capital loss. [See

Chapter 8, "Managing Your Brokerage and 401(k) Accounts," for details.]

- *Check with your company or union.* Many have scholarship programs for children of employees and often for young people who work part-time for the company. For example, McDonald's has a $1,000 scholarship program for high school seniors who work for the company at least 15 hours a week. Big Y, a supermarket chain in the Northeast, even includes its customers in its scholarship program. The AFL-CIO offers scholarships ranging from $500 to $4,000 through its Union Plus Scholarship Program. Contact your local union or visit www.unionplus.org/college-education-financing/union-plus-scholarship.

WHAT GRANDPARENTS AND OTHERS CAN DO

There are several ways in which family members and friends can participate in funding a college nest egg.

- *EE Savings Bonds,* which we described in Chapter 1, come with some nice tax benefits when they are used to pay for college, although there are income caps. *Details:* "Savings Bonds" at www.finaid.org/savings/bonds/phtml explains it all.
- *The Coverdell Education Savings Account (ESA).* Anyone can contribute up to the $2,000 a year limit from all sources to this account (formerly known as the Education IRA). Withdrawals are tax-free. To qualify (for either a full or a partial contribution), your adjusted gross income must be under $110,000 if you're single and $220,000 if you're married and filing jointly.

- *Direct payment.* Grandparents can pay tuition and college costs directly to the college—up to the full amount of all college costs—without it counting as part of the annual $12,000 gift tax exemption. However, doing so most likely will reduce financial aid.

PAYING BACK COLLEGE LOANS

Once your student has that diploma in hand, a new set of financial decisions emerge as you and your student start paying back the loans you took. The average student now graduates with about $21,000 in debt. Here are the steps that any graduate with college loans should take:

To handle your federal loans, start with the feds (www.federalstudentaid.ed.gov/locate.html). You'll get up-to-date information on how to track your loans online, along with details on repayment options and loan consolidation.

Next, visit FinAid (www.finaid.org/calculators), which has a great set of calculators that let you figure out how you'll fare in paying back most student loans.

With federal loans, options to repay your debt beyond the standard repayment plan (which generally gives you up to 10 years for federal Perkins loans and up to 25 years for Stafford loans, depending on the payment plan you select) are

Extended repayment. This gives you up to 25 years to repay your loans, but it costs significantly more in interest.

Graduated repayment. This starts out with low payment amounts. These are then increased every two years. You'll need to be fairly confident that your income will rise as time goes on.

Income-contingent or income-sensitive repayment. This calculates your payments based on your adjusted gross income and family size. Most people will wind up paying less than 10% of their total income. If you haven't fully repaid your loan in 25 years, the unpaid portion will be forgiven. If you work for a nonprofit or hold a government job, your loan may qualify for public loan service forgiveness and be forgiven after 10 years of payments. *Details:* www.ibrinfo.org. (IBRinfo is a nonprofit organization created by Project on Student Debt.)

If you are finding it almost impossible to make your loan payments because of the sour economy, you can apply for an *economic hardship deferment,* which will allow you to postpone payments under certain circumstances. Interest, however, continues to grow on nonfederally subsidized loans. If you qualify (check the FinAid Web site or www.ibrinfo.org to find out), make every effort to pay the dollar amount equal to the interest due so that you're not falling deeper into debt.

> **$ TIP**   If you've been paying back private student loans on time, you may be able to consolidate them and/or get a lower interest rate. It all depends on your FICO credit score (see Chapter 7).

THE BOTTOM LINE: Don't mess around with student loan payments. If you default, severe penalties will follow. There are no exceptions, even if you speak fluent Latin and Greek and graduated magna cum laude. For example, if you skip payments on federal loans for 270 days, the government will march right in and garnishee your wages—up to 15% of them. Plus your federal and state income tax refund may be applied to your loan.

In some states, if you are required to have a state license to operate in your field, you may be blocked from renewing it if you default. Even if you declare bankruptcy, you'll find it almost impossible to get student loans discharged. And the final bit of bad news: if you die, private lenders (with whom you can be in default if you're only 30 days late making a payment) will go after your estate.

But to end this chapter on a happy note, keep in mind that as an American with a student loan, the IRS will grant you a tax break. You can deduct the interest you pay on your loans (up to $2,500 a year) if your modified adjusted gross income is under $75,000 (for singles) or $150,000 (for marrieds filing joint returns). And the deduction can be taken for the full life of the loan.

WORDSMARTS

ADJUSTED GROSS INCOME (AGI): A tax-related figure arrived at by adding up all your income for the year to get your gross income and then subtracting adjustments. Adjustments include contributions to your qualified retirement accounts, alimony payments, qualified moving expenses, student loan interest, medical savings account deductions, and, if you're self-employed, half the self-employment tax. Once all your adjustments have been subtracted, you have your AGI.

COLLEGE BOARD: A not-for-profit membership organization founded in 1900 with headquarters in New York. It is best known for managing standardized tests, including the SAT.

MODIFIED ADJUSTED GROSS INCOME: Your AGI with certain deductions added back, such as a deduction claimed for a regular contribution to an IRA.

SALLIE MAE: The country's largest college student loan company, with more than 10 million borrowers. It provides federally guaranteed student loans and has its headquarters in Reston, Virginia.

FOR FURTHER INFORMATION

PAYING FOR COLLEGE WITHOUT GOING BROKE, by Kalman Chany (New York: Princeton Review Books, 2009). Revised annually, this is the bible in the field.

SIMPLE TUITION. Shop for loans and compare their pros and cons at www.simpletuition.com.

TUITION MANAGEMENT SYSTEMS. Covers options available to families for paying for college at www.afford.com.

BANKRATE. Saving for college at www.savingforcollege.com.

10

Helping Those of a Certain Age

"Age doesn't matter unless you're a cheese."
—BILLIE BURKE

We are an aging country, and, unfortunately, one in which many older people have recently lost huge chunks of their nest eggs in serious stock market dips and debacles like that of Enron. You may be one of them, although I sincerely hope not. This chapter has a myriad of tips on how to find work, along with ways to take advantage of the many special discounts and savings designed especially for those of a certain age.

If you've lost your job, you're undoubtedly looking for a new one—to help with the bills, make up for losses in the stock market, or fund your retirement. Or maybe you haven't worked in ages (or perhaps ever), but you want a regular paycheck so that you can enjoy the little luxuries of life—dining out more often, taking a vacation, or buying season tickets. Whatever your situation, don't fret about being of a certain age. And don't fret if you're no longer needed in what was once your field of working expertise.

Instead, think of your situation as an opportunity to do something new. Think Grandma Moses. She began painting when she was in her seventies. Before she died at age 101, she had completed 3,600 canvases, one of which, "Fourth of July," hangs in the White House and another of which, "Sugaring Off," sold for $1.2 million in 2006.

And think Rex Stout. The creator of the Nero Wolfe detective stories was the Kansas state spelling bee champion at the age of 13, a warrant officer on board President Theodore Roosevelt's yacht, a cigar store clerk, a sightseeing guide, and an itinerant bookkeeper. In this last role, he devised a school banking system that was installed in 400 cities and towns around the country. He then retired from the financial world, moved to Paris for a time, and began writing. His first novel about the larger-than-life detective was published in 1934. A month before he died in 1975 at age 88, he published his seventy-second Nero Wolfe story.

GETTING PSYCHED

Thinking ahead and doing a little research and preparation prior to your first interview will make it all the more likely that you'll be offered a position. So, take the time to read Chapter 13, "Getting Work When There Is No Work," for tips on how to actually land an interview and then ace it. Much of the information in that chapter applies to people of all ages.

If you're uncertain about what you want to do or how to go about it, begin by attending a workshop, consulting a career coach, or both. Start with the Five O'Clock Club (800-538-6645, www.

fiveoclockclub.com), an outplacement firm with a nationwide network of career counselors. The $49 per year membership also provides access to one-on-one counseling at reasonable rates. Counselors will walk you through self-assessment techniques and help you prepare a résumé and develop job search strategies.

If you do not live near a Five O'Clock Club, the National Board for Certified Counselors, Inc. (336-547-0607, www.nbcc. org) will help you find a career counselor in your area.

> **$ TIP** If you're concerned about revealing your age on your résumé, omit the dates of your education and focus on your last 10 years of work. The rest can go under "Other Experience." Be sure to put three or four sentences explaining your most outstanding qualifications at the top of the résumé.

If you're wondering what careers are in demand now and are likely to be so in the future, head for the U.S. Bureau of Labor Statistics' Employment Projection Program (www.bls. gov/emp). Here you'll find the most up-to-date *Occupational Outlook Handbook* (which lists occupations with details on expected job prospects, salaries, training and education needed, and what you actually do on a particular job) and the *Career Guide to Industries*, with links to similar information grouped by industry rather than by job.

WHERE THE JOBS ARE

Smart companies realize that ability is not age-related. The following industries and stores favor older workers because they dress appropriately, show up for work on time, are polite, don't take phony sick days, and are dedicated to doing a very good job and making their boss look good.

- *Banks.* Older workers are excellent as tellers and customer service reps.
- *Bookstores.* Those of a certain age are from a generation of readers. Bookstores, and also news and stationery stores, value their appreciation of literature, knowledge of current affairs, and enthusiasm for reading.
- *Child care.* The high number of working mothers has led to an expanding day-care/child-care industry—one to which older people bring patience, experience, and ideas.
- *Dance schools.* Can you do the tango? The waltz? The fox trot? You may get a teaching position faster than you can say cha-cha-cha.
- *Florists, nurseries, and garden shops.* Many of these businesses hire people over 50 as part-time workers to fill in during peak seasons.
- *Hardware stores.* Both the major chains and mom-and-pop operations like older workers who have fix-up and repair experience.
- *Home health care.* There's continual demand for aides, physical therapists, companions, and people to prepare and deliver meals.
- *Hotels.* Many hotels hire older men and women as desk clerks and to fill other positions.
- *Craft, sewing, and knitting stores.* People who are craft-oriented, can knit one, purl two, or can thread a bobbin make ideal employees. Some are hired to teach customers how to do the same.
- *Tax return preparers.* (See Chapter 13.)
- *Teachers and tutors.* (See Chapter 13.)

Travel. The industry often needs customer service reps and tour guides.

LEADING SOURCES FOR HELP AND IDEAS

The AARP National Employer Team (www.aarp.org) is made up of companies that are committed to recruiting older workers. In addition to many that are in the categories just listed, there are companies in the communications and financial services fields, and also with the federal government.

Among the firms (and one government employer) currently posted on the AARP Web site are

AT&T	Manpower
Avis	MetLife
Borders	Pitney Bowes
CVS	Principal Finance Group
Comcast	Staples
Home Depot	Toys"R"Us
IRS	Verizon
Kelly Services	Walgreens

Searching by type of work and location on the site is free. Go directly to www.aarp.org/jobs. And why not join the organization's discussion group, "The Water Cooler," for advice from others or to share with others. Among the current topics: looking for work, launching a new career, and dealing with age bias. It all happens at www.aarp.org/community/groups/The WaterCooler.

Next, look at Check Retirement Jobs.com (www.retirement jobs.com), where employers around the United States who are eager to recruit older workers post their openings. The site also has lots of advice on job hunting, résumé writing, and interviewing—even podcasts with experts.

Also, be sure to check with your local or state career center (see Chapter 11). It may offer workshops and counseling on how to use your age to your advantage. Your state may also have an Operation ABLE program that helps older workers train for and find jobs.

If you're a retired lawyer and you would like to get back into action, the American Bar Association's special search engine, Second Season of Service, will help you find volunteer and pro bono opportunities. Go directly to www.abanet.org/SecondSeason. (Keep in mind that volunteer work often turns into paid part-time and sometimes even full-time work.)

THE INTERVIEW AND THE THREE Es

Once you've lined up an interview, take a few minutes to consider the fact that you may be interviewed by someone who is young enough to be your son or daughter. So don't make a big thing about your age or that of the interviewer; resist saying, "Oh, you look so much like my son," or, "My daughter graduated from the same school."

Instead focus on the *three Es*: being energetic, enthusiastic, and engaging. Point out that you love a challenge. If you jog, play tennis, swim, or are a great bridge or chess player, quietly work this into the conversation. Stress your ability and willingness to learn new technology.

Although you should wear something that doesn't date you (like your old college pleated skirt with knee socks or a narrow necktie from the fifties), don't select an "in" outfit that looks attractive only on a skinny 25-year-old.

If you haven't been on an interview in recent years and are wondering how you should dress, check with friends who are in positions similar to the ones in which you are interested. For many jobs, a suit is the way to go; for some more casual environments, that may turn out to be overkill.

> **$ TIP** It's unlawful to be turned down for a job because of age, if you're 40 or older. If you feel that you've been discriminated against because of age, don't stand for it. Call the Equal Employment Opportunity Commission at 800-669-4000. It will conduct an investigation to determine if your rights have been violated.

SETTING UP YOUR OWN BUSINESS

You may decide that now is the time to start your own business. One of the least expensive and least difficult routes to take is to become a consultant based on your previous profession or job, working from a home office.

In addition to taking up painting like Grandma Moses or writing like Rex Stout, consider these home-based businesses:

- Appliance, bike, and car repair
- Bill paying, letter writing
- Catering
- Child or elder care
- Computer programming, design, management
- Delivery or messenger service
- Driving those who cannot drive to appointments

- Freelance writing and editing
- Grocery shopping and running errands for busy professionals
- House-sitting and house cleaning
- House repairs
- Lawn and garden care
- Newsletter publishing
- Pet care
- Research and clipping service

IT PAYS TO AGE

One of the nice things about being older is that there are lots of discounts for owning up to being 50, 55, 60, 62, or older. More often than not, these savings are not prominently mentioned or even advertised, so my advice is, wherever you are, always ask. Each such discount helps recession-proof your life.

And, don't think "senior discounts" (what a terrible phrase) consist only of the "early bird special" at your neighborhood restaurant, which often means dining at 4:30, which is really afternoon teatime. Here are other ways, in alphabetical order, in which it pays to age:

- *AARP.* Membership in this national organization costs $12.50 a year and brings you discounts on car rentals, cruises, fitness centers, hotels, and various retailers as well as access to auto, home, life, long-term care, and medical insurance.
- *Age-based discounts.* Other places where those who speak up get a break in price include banks (including traveler's checks), phone services, eyeglasses and contact lenses, flu shots, and dental services.

- *Airlines.* Discounts periodically come and go, depending upon the status of the industry.
- *Amtrak.* For those 62 and over, there's a 15% discount off the lowest fare on most trains. On cross-border service with VIA Rail Canada, there's a 10% discount for those 60 and over.
- *Box stores.* Discounts for seniors at places such as Kohl's, Home Depot, Target, Walgreens, and Wal-Mart come and go. But keep checking. Some such stores run "senior Tuesdays."
- *Concerts.* A number of halls and auditoriums have discounts for older people. For example, the esteemed New York (City) Philharmonic has "senior rush tickets" available on a first come, first served basis the day of the performance at Avery Fisher Hall box office.
- *Greyhound.* There is a 5% discount for those 62 or over.
- *Hotels, motels, and resorts.* Widespread and varying discounts exist for people who are 50, 55, 60, or 62 and over. For example, Marriott has a 15% for those who are 62 or older, and Choice has a 10% discount for those age 50 or older and 20% to 30% off if you're 60 or older.
- *Matinees.* Afternoon tickets for Broadway shows, baseball games and other sporting events, opera performances, and concerts are always less pricey than the same presentation in the evening.
- *Movies.* Most theaters give discounts to older people. For example, at AMC Theaters, tickets for those 60 and older are $9 rather than $10 ($12.50 in some cities) and $6 on Tuesdays.

- *Parks.* In addition to discounts at your local and state recreational areas, our National Park Service has a terrific lifetime senior pass. Called America the Beautiful, it costs $10 and provides free access to national parks and federal recreational lands for those 62 and older and a 50% discount on certain activities, such as camping.

- *Public transportation.* Almost every city and town reduces its fares on buses and subways.

- *Skiing.* Lift tickets and season passes are often discounted. For example, at Whiteface Mountain in Lake Placid, New York, those age 65 to 69 save $14 on lift tickets, and those 70 or older ski free. At Utah's Park City Mountain Resort, a season pass is $1,450, but drops to $575 for those age 65 to 69 and down to $295 if you're 70 or older.

- *Trailways.* There is a 10% discount for those 65 or older.

- *Travel companies.* Many offer 5% to 15% off on package tours for those somewhere in between 55 and 90.

THE BOTTOM LINE: Type "senior discount" into a Google search and you'll find many more. And check out two comprehensive Web sites: The Seasoned Spender (www.seasonedspender.com) and Senior Discounts (www.seniordiscounts.com).

FOR FURTHER INFORMATION

EXPERIENCE WORKS (866-397-9757, www.experienceworks.org), a nonprofit organization funded by the federal government, provides counseling, training, and paid community service assignments for low-income workers 55 and older to help them make the transition to regular employment.

HOW WORK AFFECTS YOUR SOCIAL SECURITY BENEFITS is free from your local social security office or from www.ssa.gov/pubs.

11

Anticipating the Pink Slip

*"Getting fired is nature's way of telling you that you had the
wrong job in the first place."*

—HAL LANCASTER

*Some employees have a knack for knowing what's
going on in their company and are fully in the loop.
But just as many haven't a clue. And not having a clue
means not being prepared. If any of the following is
happening in your work life, it's possible that you will
be handed a pink slip. And that possibility increases
exponentially when our economy is less than robust.
Knowing in advance that you might be fired enables
you to take practical steps to lessen the impact and
even find unexpected opportunities. This chapter tells
you how to protect your current job and the initial
steps to take in case you are laid off.*

Although experts disagree over the origin of the phrase *pink
slip*, most say that the term dates back to the early 1900s and
the practice of putting a termination notice in an employee's

pay envelope, often on a pink piece of paper so that it would not be overlooked.

RECESSION-PROOF YOUR JOB

A surprising number of people manage to keep their jobs even when everyone around them is being laid off. Here are seven "up" strategies to offset the seven reasons that you might be let go.

They center around the proven fact that, unfair as it may seem, wallflower employees rarely survive cuts in a tough economy. And if you're one of the clueless ones we mentioned earlier, be smart and acquire antennae. Find out who usually does know the inside scoop and develop or strengthen your relationship with that person. It could help save your job.

1. SHOW UP. Be there. Come in early. Stay late. Be seen in the cafeteria. Eat at your desk several times a week. Play on the company's baseball team. Participate in its charitable activities.

2. SPEAK UP. Contribute ideas to meetings. Suggest solutions. Have answers to questions at the ready. But don't speak up if it means whining about extra work assignments or longer hours.

3. ADD UP. Add up all your accomplishments. Maintain an ongoing list, and be prepared to show it to your boss or verbally discuss one or two items with him. Your supervisor may not be fully aware of your achievements or may simply be too preoccupied to notice.

4. MEET UP. Attend company meet, greet, and eat events as well as all department meetings and union get-togethers. And don't be shy—pass out your card. Contribute. Make coffee dates. Get known without being overly pushy.

5. BEEF UP. Improve your performance. Be seen as a hard worker. Prove your worth. Go for new accounts. Take on assignments. Volunteer to lead a project. Fill in a vacuum. Teach an extra class. Be indispensable. And, in the process, make your boss look good.

6. JOIN UP. Take out memberships in professional groups and networking organizations.

7. WRITE UP. Contribute items to your company's newsletter. Write a position paper. Review a book in your field. Agree to take meeting notes. Get your name in print, but not by writing negative things about your company or your boss on your blog or on Facebook.

> **$ TIP** Another write-up item is your résumé. Update it, but do so on your home computer. If you're laid off, you may not be able to retrieve it from your office.

SEVEN SIGNS THAT YOU MAY BE LET GO

Most layoffs don't just happen. They're usually preceded by a steady flow of bad news signs—bosses gathered behind closed doors, unscheduled board meetings, outsiders brought in to "fix" things.

Aside from getting swept up in an overall company layoff, you have a greater chance of being laid off if

1. YOU MADE A MAJOR, MAJOR MISTAKE. Perhaps you lost an important account. You messed up a presentation big time. You took home office supplies or equipment. You've called in sick twice too often. You don't get along with your boss or your colleagues.

2. YOUR LAST WORK REVIEW WAS POOR. If you didn't receive praise and thanks for a job well done, it could be that management is unhappy with your work, although some bosses believe that if you do something right, that's what you were hired to do and you shouldn't expect praise. Just be aware.

3. YOUR WORKLOAD HAS CHANGED. Your hours have been changed to the least desirable or the least convenient, such as the night shift or the weekend tour of duty. Or you're no longer managing other people or heading up a team. You've been moved to a smaller office. Your assignments have become less important.

4. YOUR SALARY HAS BEEN FROZEN. Or it's been cut. Or you've been asked to take a sabbatical or a buyout. However, if this has happened to everyone else in the company, it's less worrisome. Management may be trying to keep as many employees as possible.

5. YOUR IMMEDIATE SUPERVISOR WAS LET GO. If you're not promoted to fill that position or if the replacement comes in with her own team, the outlook isn't good. Or, if you learn that the department that your supervisor headed up is being reorganized, it could mean that your own position will not be there after the dust settles.

6. THE COMPANY IS CHANGING. It may be up for sale, have been sold, or be merging with another firm. These scenarios often lead to redundancy—in the new configuration, two people won't be needed to do the same job.

7. THE COMPANY IS NOT MAKING MONEY. Or it's bleeding money. Keep a check on your company's financial status by reading the annual and quarterly reports online. If it's a publicly traded firm, check its bond ratings with Moody's (www.moodys.com) and Standard & Poor's (www.standardandpoors.com). If the ratings have been lowered, it could mean that the company's financial health is looking dubious, and thus layoffs or even bankruptcy might be on the horizon. (Standard & Poor's also maintains a company credit watch.)

$ TIP To understand how bond ratings work, go to http://personal. fidelity.com/products/fixedincome/bondratings.shtml.

IMMEDIATE STEPS TO TAKE

If any one of the seven scenarios just outlined has taken place or if you hear rumors floating around your office or plant, immediately update your Rolodex, BlackBerry, or e-mail address book. Transfer any information on your office computer to your home computer. Some companies are incredibly tough and give fired employees only 30 minutes to an hour or so to collect their personal items before leaving the workplace for the last time. And fired employees are often physically escorted off the premises.

Be sure your updated address list includes the contact information for current and former colleagues and supervisors, along with clients and customers with whom you have a relationship. You'll want to tap them for personal recommendations and for leads about new positions.

And, gather up laudatory letters and e-mails from your supervisors, clients, and customers. These too will become unavailable once you're shown the door.

PREPARE TO COLLECT UNEMPLOYMENT INSURANCE

Another step you can take in anticipation of being handed a pink slip is to find out how to collect unemployment insurance. Lining up the required documents takes time, and the sooner you're on the case, the sooner you'll receive your first check. Hopefully, you won't need to apply.

This government program was set up in 1935 to give payments (by check, direct deposit, or an unemployment debit card) to workers who lose their job through no fault of their own. Payments are for a specific length of time or until you find a new job.

Your employer has been funding this government benefit over the years, and you're entitled to make use of it. Don't be shy about doing so. It will provide a much-needed short-term financial cushion.

Note: There are two common situations that are likely to make you ineligible: first, if you left your job voluntarily, and second, if your severance package includes a salary for a stated time period (rather than a lump sum). In the latter case, you would not be eligible until the payments stop. However, the rules here are vague, so file anyway and let the state tell you if you're not eligible.

How to File

Apply to your nearest state unemployment office as soon as you're officially let go—you won't receive a check until all the paperwork is complete and your eligibility has actually been verified. This could take up to three weeks, and sometimes longer.

$ TIP To find the appropriate office and filing instructions, including the required documents, go to www.servicelocator.org/OWSLinks.asp.

Each state's Web site explains how to apply—online, by phone, or by mail. Very few require you to drop into a physical office anymore.

Your state's Web site will also spell out what material is needed. New York State, for example, requires the following information; other states have similar or even additional requirements:

- Your social security number
- A valid driver's license or nondriver photo ID card number
- Your mailing address and zip code
- Your telephone number (Monday through Friday, 8 A.M. to 5 P.M.)
- Your employer's registration number or federal employer ID number
- The name, address, zip code, and telephone number of your most recent employer
- Your alien registration card if you're not a U.S. citizen
- Copies of Forms SF-8 and SF-50 if you were a federal employee in the last 18 months

- A copy of your most recent separation form, DD214, Member 4, if you are an ex-service member claiming benefits based on your military service
- For direct deposit of benefits, your bank routing and checking account numbers

How Much You'll Receive

The money you receive is provided by state unemployment insurance programs funded by a tax imposed on employers (with the exception of several states that also require a minimal employee contribution). The overall guidelines are federally determined, but the specific dollar amounts are decided at the state level.

Although the formula varies, it is based on a percentage of your earnings over the previous 52 weeks, not to exceed your state's statutory cap. For example, the weekly cap in New York State is $405; in Illinois, $369; in Mississippi, $230; and in California, $450. (Illinois also has a supplement if you have a non-working spouse or dependent children.) According to the Center for American Progress, the average unemployed worker in 2008 received $293 a week, replacing about 35% of his weekly wage.

$ TIP To check your state's formula, contact your state unemployment office; for a list of offices, go to www.servicelocator.org/OWSLinks.asp.

You'll get a check for a minimum of 26 weeks. When the unemployment rate around the country is high, this period is often extended, with additional extensions in particular states with exceptionally high unemployment. This is known as emergency unemployment compensation or extended benefits. In 2008, the federal government provided up to 20 weeks of extended benefits in all states plus up to 13 weeks in addition in high-unemployment states such as California.

The 2009 stimulus bill did not grant additional weeks of benefits but it did extend the time period in which to qualify for extended benefits. Prior to the passage of the stimulus bill, you had to run out of regular benefits before the end of March 2009 in order to be granted extended benefits. Now you have until December 31, 2009.

Unfortunately, unemployment insurance is taxed at the federal level and, in some states, at the state level. However, under the stimulus plan, the first $2,400 in unemployment compensation received in 2009 is not subject to federal tax.

FIVE REASONS YOU MIGHT NOT COLLECT UNEMPLOYMENT

(Please note the word *might*. These are determined by the state.)

1. You walked out or quit voluntarily without good cause.

2. You were fired for misconduct connected with your work.

3. You are not able, ready, and willing to accept a suitable job.

4. You refused an offer of suitable work.

5. You knowingly made false statements to get benefit payments.

Job Help

In order to collect unemployment insurance, your state may require you to register with its "job service" division and show that you are actively looking for work. Most states want to know that you are willing and available to take a suitable job if one is offered. The definition of the word *suitable* varies. Here's how Virginia defines it:

> *Many factors are taken into consideration in determining whether work is suitable. These factors include your previous work experience, your physical and mental fitness, risk to your health, safety, or morals and the distance from your home. You must report all job offers that you decline when you file your weekly claim for benefits.*

$ TIP The Department of Labor runs a career center in every state. To find the one closest to you as well as links to special programs for older workers and disabled individuals, type in your zip code at www.servicelocator.org or call 1-877-US-2-JOBS.

WORDSMARTS

BANK ROUTING NUMBER: The bank code on your check that identifies the financial institution that the money is drawn on. It consists of the first nine digits (starting on the left) at the bottom of your check.

BOND RATING: An independent grading of a company's debt securities (primarily bonds). It evaluates the issuer's ability to make interest and principal payments. The two major rating services are Moody's and Standard & Poor's.

FOR FURTHER INFORMATION

AFL-CIO. Visit this Web site even if you're not a union worker. You'll find excellent guidance on how to deal with the emotional and financial ramifications of unemployment: www.aflcio.org/issues/jobseconomy/unemployment/.

U.S. DEPARTMENT OF LABOR EMPLOYMENT AND TRAINING ADMINISTRATION; http://workforcesecurity.doleta.gov/unemploy/.

NATIONAL EMPLOYMENT LAW PROJECT; www.unemployedworkers.org/.

12

Surviving the Pink Slip

"Winners never quit and quitters never win."

—TED TURNER

No one, from clerks to CEOs, is immune from losing her job. This is true in good times as well as tough times. And when it happens, those who planned to glide into retirement are cast adrift, and those who were on the fast track are suddenly derailed. But there are solutions, as you'll read in this chapter.

Take heart. A number of famous people have been fired, including Bill Belichick, Michael Bloomberg, Bernadine Healy, Billie Jean King, Bernie Marcus, Joe Torre, Robert Redford, and Jesse Ventura. You can find out how these and other successful people never quit and managed to bounce back winners in Harvey Mackay's book *We Got Fired!*

12 STEPS TO TAKE WHEN YOU GET THE WORD

If you're one of the thousands of Americans who has been let go, you're not alone in facing a number of key financial decisions. Here's how to survive the pink slip.

Step 1:
Cash In on Your Health-Care Flexible Spending Account

If you've been contributing pretax dollars from your paycheck to a flexible spending account in order to cover unreimbursed medical expenses (such as deductibles and copayments), as soon as you know you're being let go, make an appointment to talk with your benefits officer.

In many cases, money left in this plan at the end of the year goes to your employer, not to you. This is informally known as the "use it or lose it" rule. The use it or lose it rule may also kick in if you leave your job, or it may not. But you need to find out.

WAYS TO USE UP YOUR HEALTH-CARE FLEXIBLE SPENDING ACCOUNT

Annual medical exam	Eye exams
Braces (dental)	Eyeglasses
Certain over-the-counter medications	Eye procedures such as Lasik surgery
Contact lenses	Flu and pneumonia shots
Copayments for out-of-network doctors	Hearing aids
	Prescription drugs
Dental exams and procedures that are not covered	Smoking cessation programs
	Weight loss programs

Step 2:
Prepare for Your Exit Interview

As we described in Chapter 11, the terms of your departure could affect your unemployment benefits. You're eligible for benefits if you lost your job through no fault of your own. If there's any question about this or any gray areas, clear them up in your exit interview. You want it to be 100% clear that you were laid off for economic reasons.

Step 3:
Find Out about Benefits

The human resources department or your boss should be able to tell you the benefits to which you're entitled. Your discussion checklist should include severance pay, accrued vacation days, overtime, sick pay, pension benefits, life insurance, health insurance, and eligibility for unemployment insurance. Take notes during your meeting, or tape-record the session, and insist on information on each item.

Step 4:
Get Letters of Reference

Ask your boss or supervisor for a letter of reference. Press (nicely) right away while he may be feeling sorry, perhaps even guilty, that you're being fired—and while your accomplishments and work history are still fresh in his mind. Your boss may even spontaneously offer the name of a contact or call a potential employer on your behalf.

Step 5:
File Papers to Keep Your Health Insurance

Whether you're employed or temporarily unemployed, after paying your mortgage or rent, health insurance should be next on your bills-to-be-paid list. And thanks to the Consolidated Omnibus Budget Reconciliation Act of 1985 (COBRA), companies with 20 people or more must offer employees who are being laid off the opportunity to extend their health coverage at group rates. The continued coverage lasts a minimum of 18 months and sometimes longer.

That's the good news. The bad news is that under normal circumstances you are the one who has to pay the premiums—100% of them plus an administrative fee. According to the Kaiser Family Foundation, in 2008 the average premium was $397 per month for an individual and $1,081 for a family. If you've been accustomed to your employer paying all or most of your premiums, this may come as a bit of a shock.

However, under the 2009 stimulus act, people who sign up for COBRA will have to pay only 35% of the premium! The federal government will reimburse employers (or health plans) for the other 65% for up to nine months.

To qualify, you had to involuntarily leave your job between September 1, 2008 and December 31, 2009. This nice break phases out between $125,000 and $145,000 in adjusted gross income for singles and between $250,000 to $290,000 for married couples filing jointly.

The reduction in the cost of your premium can also cover your spouse, partner, or dependents who were in your health plan. However, you cannot get the subsidy if you are eligible for another group plan, such as your spouse's, or for Medicare.

$ TIP If you lost your job after September 1, 2008 and declined COBRA, you now get another chance to enroll. Check with your former employer.

With or without the stimulus subsidy, COBRA premiums are almost always less than you would pay if you took out your own individual health insurance policy. There are two possible exceptions to this: If your spouse has coverage, it's probably cheaper to purchase family coverage under her plan. And if you're very young and very healthy, your own plan might be cheaper than your employer-provided plan.

$ TIP To check on what your state offers, visit the National Association of Health Underwriters Web site, http://www.nahu.org. Click on "Consumer Education."

! CAUTION: You must apply within 60 days after being notified by your employer of your rights under COBRA, and you have 45 days after you elect COBRA coverage to make the first premium payment.

If you think you will land a new job right away, the 60 days is important: it means that you can postpone paying COBRA premiums for two months and still be covered. But watch the calendar like a hawk, especially if you have a preexisting medical condition. If you go over the 60 days without insurance and then get a job that has employee insurance, the new company's health plan is not obligated to cover your preexisting medical condition.

And *COBRA is not universal.* The federal government has its own form of continuation coverage for its employees (similar to COBRA), and many states have "mini-COBRA" plans that cover employees of smaller companies (those with 2 to 19 employees). Ask.

If you have a health plan through a church or church-related association, you may not be able to apply for COBRA, although other continuation programs that are very similar to COBRA are often available. Again, ask.

Nor is COBRA available to those who are fired for gross misconduct. The definition of gross misconduct is vague, but it is likely to include theft, embezzlement, violation of company policy, and non-work-related violence affecting the workplace. So behave.

Step 6: Play the Guilt Card

If you've been a loyal worker, the company may feel guilty about letting you go. Don't be shy about using this to negotiate rather than merely accepting the departing perks that are offered. You should try to get a better severance package than the one that is initially offered, as well as outplacement services (or funds for such services) or the use of an office, computer, and phone to help you search for a new job.

Or negotiate for freelance or consulting work; this is often possible when someone is let go because the company can't afford a full-time employee, not because it's unhappy with the person's work.

If you're a top-level executive, you may want to hire a specialist to negotiate for you.

$ TIP To find a lawyer specializing in employment issues, go to the National Employment Lawyer Association (http://www.nela.org/ NELA) or use links to state-specific sources at the American Bar Association Web site, www.abalawinfo.org/find1.html.

Step 7: Be Nice

This involves writing a letter to the head of your old company. (Keep a copy for your files.) Explain how much you enjoyed working there for however many years, that you were pleased to be part of the department or team, and that you hope to reconnect in the future. Not only will this letter be helpful when you ask your former boss for a reference, but it will also boost the likelihood of your being rehired if and when the company rebounds.

Step 8: Hang Up Your Bathrobe

Once you no longer have an office or plant to go to every day, you may be tempted to stay home and hang out in your bathrobe. Don't. It's a bad idea. In addition to looking for work, set up a daily morning walk or jog (with a friend so that you'll keep the commitment). Or sign up for classes at a gym or your local Y. Many people keep focused and find support in morning exercise, meditation, tai chi, or prayer groups.

Former employees of a company often organize their own support groups; find out if this is the case with your old firm, and if so, join in.

Until you have a job, treat job hunting as a full-time 9-to-5 job. Get dressed as though you were going to an office (minus the necktie or high heels) and keep the same hours, giving yourself 60 minutes for lunch and then going right back to the job of finding a job until it's time to quit at 5 P.M. You'll find that persistence pays off.

Finally, don't panic. Problems come with solutions. And despite layoffs, there are always employers seeking employees. It may take you a while to find the type of work you like, you may have to compromise somewhat, or this may be the time for you to shift gears and change your career. (See Chapter 13, "Getting Work When There Is No Work.")

Step 9: Make a Realistic Budget and Stick to It

Prepare for leaner times. That means skipping nonessentials, cutting back on luxury items, eating out less, carpooling, and taking the bus or walking instead of jumping into taxis. And giving up those cappuccinos-to-go at $3.75 each.

(See Chapter 3, "Buttoning Down," for tips on saving money and drawing up a frugal budget.)

Step 10: Be Straight with Your Kids

Tell your children you're out of work. If you try to hide the fact, they may imagine that something much worse is going on—kids always sense tension at home. Explain what happened, what steps you are taking to find a new job, and what they can expect—such as that they may be going to day camp rather than sleepaway or they may be going to public rather than private school. And if they're old enough, ask them for suggestions. Involving them in a constructive, nonfrightening way also teaches them how to handle change and take control of difficult situations.

Step 11: Put Any Severance Pay in a Liquid Account

Your best bet is a money market fund or short-term bank CD.

Note: If you are given the choice of taking your severance pay in a lump sum or in periodic payments, it's usually better to opt for a lump sum so that you can invest the money and start earning interest right away.

If you sense that your old firm is in financial jeopardy, the decision is a no-brainer: take the money and run—to the bank. If you worked for a publicly traded company, check to see if Moody's (www.moodys.com) or Standard & Poor's (www.stand ardandpoors.com) has downgraded its bonds. If so, you can assume that the company is experiencing financial problems.

Step 12: Decide What to Do with Your 401(k)

If you have a company-sponsored retirement plan, you now must make one of four decisions: (1) you can leave the money with your old company, (2) you can roll it over into an IRA, (3) you can roll it over into a new employer's 401(k) plan, provided the new company allows rollovers, or (4) you can take it in a lump sum.

First, check with your employer. How much is in your account will determine to some extent what will happen to it when you leave the company.

For amounts of less than $1,000, the plan is allowed to just send you the money. For amounts of $1,000 or more, the plan must put a distribution from the account into a qualified IRA. If the amount is at least $1,000 but less than $5,000, the plan can distribute it (i.e., cash out your account) without first getting your agreement. But you do get notified and have a chance to choose the IRA into which it is placed. If you don't, the plan will choose an IRA for you.

OPTION 1: LEAVING YOUR 401(k) IN PLACE

This might be the right decision if you're near age 55 or older. If you retire, quit, or are fired at age 55, you can start taking regular 401(k) withdrawals or you can take out the whole amount without being hit with the standard 10% early withdrawal penalty. (The standard 10% early withdrawal penalty normally applies to those participants who withdraw money before age 59½.)

Note: This exception applies if you leave your job any time during the calendar year in which you turn 55 or later. Keep in mind that this exemption from the early withdrawal penalty applies only to 401(k)s. IRAs operate under different rules, so if you retire and roll money from your 401(k) into an IRA before age 59½, you will lose this exemption on those dollars.

$ TIP The 401(k) Help Center has full details on this complicated ruling: www.401khelpcenter.com.

Leaving your 401(k) in place also makes sense if your plan has performed well and if it has a number of investment options and low expenses. This is especially true if your new employer doesn't offer a 401(k) plan. However, find out how easily you can get your money out of your old plan should you decide later on that you want to take a lump-sum distribution or to make a rollover. Some plans have myriads of restrictive rules.

OPTION 2: ROLLING YOUR 401(k) INTO AN IRA

For the vast majority of people who are leaving their jobs, this is the wisest choice. If you select the rollover, be sure to arrange for a trustee-to-trustee transfer. Then the money goes directly from your old retirement account into an IRA.

If instead of doing a trustee-to-trustee rollover, you take the money directly (as in a lump-sum distribution), you face two tough IRS rulings. One of them allows you only 60 days to get the money into an IRA. The second requires that your former plan administrator withhold 20% for taxes.

Unless you can make up the withheld 20% from money you have elsewhere and do so within the 60-day limit, only 80% (the amount you already put into an IRA) of your eligible distribution will be tax-deferred. After 60 days, the 20% that was withheld is treated as a taxable distribution.

For example, if you have $50,000 in your 401(k), and you ask for a check in your name, the plan administrator will automatically take out 20% for taxes. That leaves you with $40,000. If you do not put that amount into an IRA within 60 days, and you're under 59½, you'll be hit with a 10% tax penalty, or $5,000. So now you'll have only $35,000.

$ TIP If your present 401(k) has few investment options (one stock fund, for example), rolling it over into an IRA might be smart—you'll have many more choices.

THE BOTTOM LINE: A trustee-to-trustee transfer protects your money from the IRS. *Note:* If you still decide to take the money yourself, keep in mind that the IRS allows only one rollover every 12 months.

Taking an immediate distribution may solve a short-term cash flow problem, but *only* if you're sure you can replace the money in time to get it into an IRA within 60 days.

OPTION 3: ROLLING OVER YOUR 401(k) INTO YOUR NEW EMPLOYER'S 401(k)

First, ask to see a five-year and a current year-to-date performance record for your new company's fund. If it did not do as well as your old company's plan, forget about this option.

On the other hand, if your new employer's plan had a superior performance record and you want to move your money, check to see if there's a waiting period before you can join the plan. If so, leave your money in your old employer's plan until that date.

Then, when you do take out your money, ask that the rollover check be written to the new plan administrator, not to you. As explained earlier, if the check is made out in your name, the administrator will deduct 20% for taxes. You then must come up with the dollar amount of that 20% in order to avoid being taxed on that amount. You will receive the 20% as a tax overpayment when you file your income tax return at the end of the year—but only if you roll over all of your money within 60 days.

OPTION 4: TAKING YOUR 401(k) IN A LUMP SUM

Most people, especially those who have lost their jobs, who take a lump sum do not put the money into an IRA or other qualified account. Instead, they use the money to live on until they get a new position. Some race right out and buy Harleys, houses, and horses.

That's not a wise decision.

$ TIP If you have high-interest debt (including credit card debt), taking a loan from your 401(k) to pay down these obligations is preferable to taking a lump sum that you might never replace. (See Chapter 4: "Tapping into Your Assets," for various ways to pay down debt without losing your retirement nest egg.

SHORT-TERM OR TEMPORARY HEALTH INSURANCE

If you don't qualify for COBRA or if your COBRA runs out before you land a new job, you will need to purchase a short-term or temporary medical insurance policy. It's dangerous to walk around without coverage. Most short-term policies run 6, 12, or sometimes up to 36 months. They typically exclude people with preexisting conditions, and rates vary widely, depending upon your age, the state where you live, whether or not you smoke, the deductible you select, and other factors. Think in terms of $100 to $300 or more per month. Among the leading companies are

Assurant Health: www.assuranthealth.com

JLBG Health: www.jlbghealth.com

United Health One: www.unitedhealthone.com

Note: Coverage on a monthly basis (for 30, 60, 90, or 180 days) is available in some states from Anthem Blue Cross Blue Shield (www.anthem.com) and Celtic Insurance (www.celtic net.com). In most cases, you must pay the deductible for the entire coverage period up front.

In addition, you can search for short-term coverage via

eHealth Insurance (www.ehealthinsurance.com), which will link you to plans for individuals, families, and small businesses. Simply answer the questions about gender, age, tobacco use, whether or not the applicant is a full-time college student, and if a spouse and children are to be included. Then put in your zip code. You will receive a list of the insurers in your area who offer coverage. Similar information is available from Short Term Medical Insurance (www.shorttermhealth.com).

$ TIP Many trade and professional associations (such as the Editorial Freelancers Association, www.the-efa.org) offer group-rate health insurance to members, as do community and religious organizations.

STEPS TO TAKE
WHEN YOU'RE LAID OFF
Check off each of these steps as you complete it.

☐ Count your money (see Chapter 1)

☐ Protect your money (see Chapter 2)

☐ Prioritize your expenses (see Chapter 3)

☐ Scale back (see Chapter 3)

☐ Conserve cash (see Chapter 3)

☐ Contact lenders (see Chapter 7)

☐ Pay down your debt (see Chapter 7)

☐ Get help (see Chapter 7)

WordSmarts

COBRA: Federal legislation requiring large employers to continue to offer group health insurance coverage, at the employee's expense, for up to 18 months after the employee is laid off. It applies only to companies with 20 or more employees.

401(K) PLAN: A type of retirement savings plan that many companies offer for their employees. The employees' contributions are exempt from federal and state income taxes until the money is withdrawn. Many companies match their employees' contributions.

403(B) PLAN: A type of retirement savings plan that is similar to a 401(k) plan, but is designed for the employees of nonprofit organizations.

457 PLAN: A type of retirement savings plan that is similar to a 401(k) plan, but is designed for state and local employees (firefighters, police officers, municipal employees) and others.

IRA ROLLOVER: A technique that allows employees to avoid taxes by transferring lump-sum payments from a 401(k) or another retirement plan into an IRA.

FOR FURTHER INFORMATION

COBRA HEALTH PLAN ADVICE FOR INDIVIDUALS & SMALL BUSINESSES: www.cobrahealth.com.

EMPLOYEE BENEFITS SECURITY ADMINISTRATION, U.S. DEPARTMENT OF LABOR: http://www.dol.gov/ebsa/consumer_info_health.html.

NATIONAL ASSOCIATION OF HEALTH UNDERWRITERS: www.nahu.org/consumer/healthcare/.

13

Getting Work When There Is No Work

*"Choose a job you love and you will never have
to work a day in your life."*
—CONFUCIUS

In tough times, many companies lay off full-time employees (albeit sometimes for limited time periods) and fill in with temporary help. That means that you may find it much easier to get a freelance or part-time job than a full-time position. Here are some little-known ways to start getting a paycheck again.

LANDING A PART-TIME JOB

Among the skills that companies look for when hiring part-timers are accounting, bookkeeping, computer programming, editing, graphic design, office assistant, repair of office equipment, telephone answering, and order fulfillment and writing. But of course, there are always other empty positions. Ideally, you'll find a job, as Confucius advised, in a field that you really like.

Incidentally, Confucius, unlike film star Jackie Coogan, apparently didn't work terribly hard. To quote Wikipedia: "Modern historians do not believe that any specific documents can be said to have been written by Confucius." Coogan, on the other hand, started working at age three when he made the first of his more than 60 films. He was also the youngest person to accumulate a million dollars and the first star to be heavily merchandised, with his own line of peanut butter, stationery, whistles, dolls, records, and figurines. You may remember him as Charlie Chaplin's sidekick in the 1920s film *The Kid*.

And Coogan accomplished all this while working part-time. He never held a 9-to-5 job.

EIGHT SIMPLE-TO-FOLLOW SUGGESTIONS

1. Want Ads

Begin by looking at the help wanted ads in your local newspaper, checking under categories that are of interest to you and/or those in which you've had previous experience. Some papers also have a "part-time" category.

Also, go to www.CraigsList.org and click on "Gigs," then on your city or town. You'll find listings for jobs involving domestic and office cleaning, moving, events and happenings, writing, designing, computers, driving vehicles, and more.

2. Local Businesses

Then contact businesses in your area that traditionally hire part-time workers, such as fast-food stores; hotels, motels, and restaurants; and institutions that care for the elderly, the terminally ill, or those undergoing rehab. Also try family-run businesses, such as clothing boutiques, opticians, hardware stores, drugstores, hair salons, nurseries, florists, and variety stores.

Schools should be next on your list. They use part-timers as crossing guards, as bus drivers, in their cafeterias, and as substitute teachers. Perhaps you qualify to be a part-time instructor at a community college or a YMCA/YWCA. These institutions teach a variety of subjects, including English as a second language, computer skills, bridge, cooking, early childhood education, dance, accounting, investing, money management for small businesses, presentation skills, résumé writing, and drawing, painting, and sculpture.

The health-care field continually needs workers for hospitals, clinics, nursing homes, and extended living facilities as well as in doctor's offices, laboratories, and patients' homes.

If you have a good driving record, you're in luck. Drivers are always needed for limousines, car services, and medical transport vehicles.

$ TIP In addition to contacting local companies, go to www.Retire mentJobs.com. Type in your zip code and the word *driver* to find listings.

3. Think Seasonally

During the December holidays, retail stores (Wal-Mart, Macy's, Gap, Target, and J.C. Penney) need extra workers. So do museum gift shops. Resorts hire additional workers during the ski season and again during the summer for positions in their restaurants, hotels, and spas, and also to give ski, tennis, swimming, horseback riding, and sailing instructions. Florists need extra help around Christmas, Valentine's Day, and Mother's Day.

This is also when delivery and messenger services hire extra drivers. In addition to thinking locally, check with FedEx, UPS, and DHL.

If you've a jolly disposition and love being around children, stores and malls can always use an extra Santa Claus.

Come January, tax preparers need people with accounting skills or simply to answer the phone and do secretarial work. H&R Block, for example, hires seasonal and part-time tax preparers, yet it also has many offices around the country that are open all year.

If you live in a college town, you might be able to take over work that students abandon when they go home for holidays and for the summer. Think waiter, busboy, theater ticket taker/usher, babysitter or pet sitter for faculty, sales assistant, grocery clerk, and delivery person.

Catering companies regularly hire workers, but especially during party season (Christmas, Hanukkah, Fourth of July, New Year's Eve, Labor Day, Thanksgiving). Take a course so that you qualify as a bartender. Or find out what training you would need to be a chef's assistant or waitperson.

$ TIP Working in the food, wine, and restaurant business usually means free food or discounts. For example, all Starbucks employees receive one pound of coffee per week as well as discounted Starbucks merchandise.

Gift shop and department store employees also make out well. If you work in one of the shops at the Metropolitan Museum of Art in New York City, you're entitled to 25% off on items that are actually sold in these shops—more during certain seasons. Macy's gives employees 20% off on in-store, catalog, and online merchandise, plus additional discounts on periodic "Employee Appreciation Days."

4. Get Paid for Doing What You Love

This is also known as turning your hobby into money. If you are artistic, why not paint portraits of babies, children, pets, or even a flattering view of a beloved home? Do the same if photography is your love. Or, paint the inside and/or outside of houses if you are a skilled housepainter.

Find out about selling your home-baked pies, cakes, and cookies. Possible outlets include caterers and local restaurants, especially coffee shops. Or get permission to sell morning or afternoon coffee and pastries in local offices.

Parents always need help at birthday parties. This is a good source of extra income for those who do magic tricks, sing, and paint faces.

If you play the piano, the cello, or another musical instrument, get out the word that you're willing to give lessons to children and/or adults. Or advertise your services for weddings, anniversaries, bar and bat mitzvahs, and other events.

Post your ad on community bulletin boards, such as at local grocery stores, the Y, and your library; include removable slips of paper with your phone number and e-mail address.

5. Become a Tutor

Remember Anna, the tutor in *The King and I*, a 1951 Broadway musical and 1956 film starring Yul Brynner as the king? Anna had a fascinating time teaching English and British customs to the king's many children and wives. (Rex Harrison played the king in a 1946 film based on the same book, *Anna and the King of Siam*, and Jodie Foster was Anna in a 1999 film also based on the book, *Anna and the King*.)

If you have a computer and reliable Internet access, you can tutor students from around the world from your home. You might not be tutoring royals, but then again you might be.

If you can commit at least nine hours a week, check out SMARTHINKING (888-430-7429, www.smarthinking.com). (Notice the one *t* in the name.) This firm hires individuals to tutor online students from schools, colleges, universities, libraries, government agencies, and textbook publishers. Candidates get paid to complete the required 10- to 15-hour online training program. And if you get a position, you'll be paid for your scheduled time even if your student cuts class.

Current open positions include such subjects as accounting, advanced statistics, biology, chemistry, economics, math beyond calculus, online writing lab, and Spanish. (*Note*: The company hires year round, but the peak hiring season is May–August and November–December.)

Another leader in the field is Tutor.com (877-724-2700,

www.tutor.com), which provides online homework help for kids in elementary school through the first year of college. Subjects include English, math, science, and social studies. Candidates must either be enrolled in or have graduated from a U.S. or Canadian college or university. You'll also need to pass an exam in the subject you want to tutor, undergo education and criminal background checks, and complete a 30- to 60-day probation period.

Preference is given to those who can commit to five hours a week, Sunday through Thursday, 4 P.M. to 11 P.M.

If you have a postgraduate degree in math, English, physics, statistics, chemistry, or biology and have at least four hours a day available, get in touch with TutorVista.com (www.tutor vista.com). TutorVista hires full- and part-time tutors to teach kindergarten through undergraduate-level subjects. For some topics, an additional degree in education is also required. Tutoring is done interactively, so you will also need a digital pen and pad.

6. Turn to a Temp Agency

Get in touch with the temp agencies listed in your Yellow Pages. Temps very often become part- or full-time employees. Manpower, for example, which has offices around the world, handles part-time permanent and temporary positions. Find the telephone number for your local office in your phone book or at www.manpower.com. The Web site supplies contact information for each branch.

Kelly Services also recruits people for contract and seasonal positions around the world. Among the fields it covers are science, law, education, health care, IT/technology, engineering, and many others. Check "Job Search" at www.kellyservices.com.

7. Go Online

Online services can be very helpful and right up to date. For example, AARP and RetirementJobs.com have joined forces to help people 50 and over find part-time work. At www.aarp.org/jobs, searching by type of work and location is free.

The national franchise 10 til 2 (877-999-1022, www.tentiltwo.com) helps people who have had at least one year of college find part-time positions, also for free.

Mom Corps (888-438-8122, www.momcorps.com) assists women in finding part-time work and contract-based assignments. There's no charge for posting your résumé.

If you have been an executive or have marketing or accounting skills, get in touch with Flexible Executives (404-255-2500, www.flexibleexecutives.com). There's a one-time fee of $300.

8. Volunteer

Finally, consider volunteering at a nonprofit organization, such as a museum, historical society, zoo, aquarium, or one of the associations working to save our forests, farmland, animals, and water. Be sure to make it known that if a part- or full-time position opens up, you wish to be considered. If you're well suited to the work, it's very likely that you will be hired for a paying position. A known employee, if he is good, is always favored over an unknown one.

THE TOP EMPLOYERS TO WORK FOR

In January, *Fortune* magazine publishes a list of the top 100 companies for which to work. Companies on the list must have at least 1,000 employees and be at least seven years old. The ranking process bases two-thirds of its review on an employee survey given to 400 employees at each company. It measures levels of trust, pride, and camaraderie.

Contact information; pay levels for the most common salaried and hourly positions, along with what those positions are; "work-life" particulars (such as whether job sharing is available); how many new jobs are posted in one year; and other details are listed for each company.

You can assume, for the most part, that these are financially healthy firms that continually or at least periodically hire workers.

Here are the top 25 for 2009:

1. Network Appliance	13. Devon Energy
2. Edward Jones	14. Robert W. Baird
3. Boston Consulting Group	15. W. L. Gore & Associates
4. Google	16. Qualcomm
5. Wegmans Food Markets	17. Principal Financial Group
6. Cisco systems	18. Shared Technologies
7. Genentech	19. OhioHealth
8. Methodist Hospital System	20. SAS
9. Goldman Sachs	21. Arnold & Porter
10. Nuggett Market	22. Whole Foods Market
11. Adobe systems,	23. Zappos.com
12. REI	24. Starbucks

25. Johnson Financial

$ TIP If you missed picking up a copy on the newsstand, check your public library or go to www.money.cnn.com/magazines/fortune/bestcompanies/2008/full_list.

THE TOP COMPANIES FOR MOTHERS

In April, *Working Mother* magazine publishes a list of companies with a work culture that is favorable to women with small children. The winners offer such things as paid sick leave, flextime, phase-back programs for new moms, adoption assistance, and paid time off to do volunteering—and in some cases even penalize the managers of employees who don't take all their vacation time!

Here are the top 25 for 2009:

1. Abbott	13. BlueCross BlueShield of North Carolina
2. Accenture	14. Bon Secours Richmond Health System
3. Allstate	15. Booz Allen Hamilton
4. American Electric Power	16. Boston Consulting Group
5. American Express	17. Bristol-Myers Squibb
6. Arnold & Porter LLP	18. Bronson
7. Arnold	19. Capital One
8. AstraZeneca	20. Children's Healthcare of Atlanta
9. Bain & Company	21. Children's Memorial Hospital
10. Bank of America	22. Chrysler
11. Baptist Health South Florida	23. Citi
12. Bayer	24. CJW Medical Center

25. Colgate-Palmolive

ACING THE INTERVIEW

You've undoubtedly found plenty of information on the Internet and in books about updating your résumé, networking, and getting your foot in the door. So, instead of covering the already well covered, here are 10 tips that you may not have read about elsewhere.

1. THINK ABOUT WHOM YOU KNOW. It's much easier to get an interview if you know someone at the company—a board member, an executive, or a lower-level employee. And don't forget about someone who is a supplier or a consultant or who does business with the firm. Ask that person to put in a good word for you.

If you get an interview, go back to your contact for advice. Find out if she knows the person who will be interviewing you, what the hot topics are, what you should wear, and what to talk about and what not to talk about. This person will also be able to help you interpret the interview afterwards.

2. MEMORIZE THREE FACTS. Research the company, institution, firm, or store in advance through its annual report or through Google. Be ready to mention three unusual or outstanding facts about the organization that caught your attention—facts that are complimentary. For example, the business is 47 years old, was founded by the immigrant grandfather of the current CEO, and is number one in its field and why. Or, that it has the most diverse workforce, teachers, or student body among its peers.

3. SHOW YOUR GOOD SIDE. More and more companies are adopting altruistic attitudes—thinking green (environmentally green, that is)—and generally gearing toward giving back to their community and the world.

Biking to work or driving an environmentally friendly vehicle will look good—unless you're applying for a job with an automobile manufacturer that produces only gas-guzzlers.

Be sure to mention any volunteer work you do or have done. If you're on a board or committee of a nonprofit organization or educational institution, let it be known.

If you're in a pickup band, play in an orchestra, or sing in a choir, find a way to mention it; likewise, mention it if you teach or coach part-time.

4. EXPLAIN YOUR NOT-SO-GOOD SIDE. If you've held a number of jobs, be prepared to explain why. If you were fired, let it be known why, keeping in mind that in a sluggish economy, this is not unexpected and not a negative. Write out answers in advance to these and any other difficult questions you anticipate. Read the answers to a savvy friend.

5. USE THE WORD WE THREE TIMES AS OFTEN AS I. This is extremely important if the job you're applying for involves teamwork, being in a small, close-knit department, or even being the personal assistant to a top executive. Inventors, writers, chemists, and bookkeepers can sometimes get away with being solo operators, but most jobs involve getting along with at least a handful of people.

6. EXPRESS A WILLINGNESS TO LEARN. Although you must showcase your knowledge and skills, don't come across as a know-it-all. (Actually, the person interviewing you may think that he knows it all—or at least that he knows more than you do.) Indicate that you like learning and are willing to return to school or take refresher courses.

7. LOOK NICE. Dress appropriately. For women, that means no cleavage or undies showing (unless you're applying for a job at Hooters). For men, it means a dress shirt rather than a tight T-shirt with the sleeves rolled up à la James Dean (unless you're looking for a job as a construction worker or as a James Dean look-alike—and even then, a dress shirt will make a better impression). If it's a firm where men wear jackets or blazers, you should do the same. It's unlikely that you're being hired to be a renegade.

And make sure your nails are clean and that you smell good.

But go easy on strong perfume or aftershave. In fact, it may be wise to avoid them altogether. Your interviewer may be scent-sensitive or have asthma or allergies.

8. TALK NICE. Aim to speak in complete sentences, and say "yes" rather than "yeah." Refrain from sounding as though you're on your cell phone, and leave at the door such "today" phrases as "oh my Gawd," "awesome," "I can't believe it," "I mean it was so cool," "no way," and "it was like . . ."

9. SIT UP STRAIGHT. But not so rigidly straight that it looks as if this is the first time you've done so. Have a firm handshake, make eye contact, and try not to fidget. Take care not to overstay your time, and smile when you leave.

10. MENTION SOMETHING CURRENT AND SOMETHING OLD-FASHIONED. You want your interviewer to realize that you are up to speed about the company or institution, trends in the field, new research, emerging products, changing methods, avant garde advertising and fund-raising techniques, and the like.

But if your interviewer is older than you are (or if you sense that it's appropriate, possibly because the interviewer alluded to a similar topic during your meeting), refer to something old-fashioned or historic. You could mention that you like F. Scott Fitzgerald's novels, early John Wayne movies, the British Museum, or Ty Cobb and baseball memorabilia. If you drop into the conversation that you spend time at your library, that always comes across as a winner.

But don't exaggerate—if you haven't read *The Iliad* and *The Odyssey*, don't mention them. Your interviewer may be an expert on ancient Greek literature and ask you to explain Nestor's role in both volumes.

Finally, handwrite an old-fashioned thank-you note on good paper—even if all your previous communication has been by phone, fax, and e-mail. It will set you apart.

DEDUCTING JOB-HUNTING EXPENSES

As soon as you start your job search, keep track of the expenses involved. Many of them may be deductible from your taxable income under the category "miscellaneous itemized deductions."

However, not everyone who is job hunting qualifies for the deductions. You must be looking for a job in the same field in which you were previously employed. And it can't be after taking "a substantial break" to board a freighter for a cruise around the world. Your search must be within a reasonable amount of time after you lost or left your previous job. And, unfortunately, if this is your first job search, you're out of luck. The IRS allows write-offs only for the expenses involved in searching for another job in your present occupation.

Keep all receipts. Then itemize them on Schedule A and attach it to your 1040.

! CAUTION You can subtract your job-hunting expenses from your income only if they add up to more than 2% of your adjusted gross income (AGI). For example, if your AGI is $50,000 and you have $1,500 in appropriate expenses, only $500 is deductible. That's $1,500 minus $1,000 (2% of $50,000). And, your job hunt need not be successful to take the tax break!

$ TIP For full details, read IRS Publication 529, "Miscellaneous Deductions." Download it at www.irs.gov or call 800-829-3676 to order a copy.

TAX-DEDUCTIBLE JOB-HUNTING EXPENSES

- Employment agency fees
- Career counseling fees
- Local and long distance phone calls
- Outplacement services
- Printing and mailing of search letters
- Printing and mailing of your résumé
- Résumé preparation help
- Start-up business costs

- Telephone calls

- Travel expenses to and from job interviews

- Want ads in newspapers and journals

- Moving expenses if you are starting a new job at least 50 miles away

Note: If you are going to an out-of-town interview, your train or plane tickets, hotels, meals, taxis, and miscellaneous expenses are deductible. But don't try to turn your trip into a vacation and deduct the full amount. This is something that the IRS watches very closely.

And, if you start your own business, certain expenses are deductible. For details, read IRS Publication 535, "Business Expenses."

WORDSMARTS

ADJUSTED GROSS INCOME (AGI): A tax-related figure arrived at by adding up all your income for the year to get your gross income and then subtracting adjustments. Adjustments include contributions to your qualified retirement accounts, alimony payments, qualified moving expenses, student loan interest, medical savings account deductions, and, if you're self-employed, half the self-employment tax. Once all your adjustments have been subtracted, you have your AGI.

DEDUCTION: An expense that you may subtract from your income to lower your taxable income. Deductions include mortgage interest, property taxes, charitable contributions, many retirement account contributions, and qualified job-hunting expenses.

FOR YOUR INFORMATION

POWERFUL SECRET IN GETTING THE JOB YOU WANT, by AndrT McIntosh (Bloomington, Ind.: AuthorHouse, 2008).

201 BEST QUESTIONS TO ASK ON YOUR INTERVIEW, by John Kador (New York, N.Y.: McGraw-Hill, 2002).

24 HOURS TO THE PERFECT INTERVIEW, by Matthew J. DeLuca (New York, N.Y.: McGraw-Hill, 2004).

14

Having Fun:
It's Chic to Be Cheap

"We are all here for a spell; get all the good laughs you can."
—WILL ROGERS

Welcome to the Age of Frugality! Conspicuous consumption is out, and saving is in. Even our president has put a cap on the salaries of executives whose companies want federal bailout money. But frugality doesn't eliminate having fun. It just means thinking in a new way—thinking in the way that the thousands of Americans that author/TV commentator Tom Brokaw called "our Greatest Generation" thought. People in the 1930s went to the movies (Will Rogers was the top-paid Hollywood movie star in the mid-1930s, earning $100,000 a picture), checked books out of their public libraries, and turned picnics into a national pastime.

Here are 20 tips for scaling down, giving up binge buying, and living life knowing that it's chic to be cheap.

EATING OUT/EATING IN

1. EAT IN. If you don't have time to cook or you always burn the toast, pick up food at your local Chinese or other inexpensive restaurant rather than dining there. You'll save at least 15% because you won't have to tip the waiter or pay for soft drinks, wine, or beer. And you'll probably have leftovers for another meal.

Great cooks "of a certain age" learned well before the recession that they could entertain just as brilliantly with the delicious entrées that stores like Costco and Trader Joe's sell. Whether it's pizza, pasta, quiche, or dips, you can let someone else do the cooking economically, while you do the reheating—and enjoying your guest.

2. GO POTLUCK. Make the old-fashioned covered-dish supper a regular habit for your circle of friends. Pick a television show that you and friends love and rotate living rooms for an evening of in-home dining and communal watching. (Ditto for Wimbledon, the Masters, the Olympics, and the World Series.)

3. DO BREAKFAST. If you do have the urge to dine out, go for breakfast. It's 50 to 80% cheaper than lunch or dinner. And take a Ziploc bag for the extra muffins. Restaurants are required by health regulations to toss out bread that's taken back to the kitchen, so you might as well toss it, too—but into your own plastic bag.

4. DINE DISCOUNT. Check out the various discount dining programs. Among the best are

REWARDS NETWORK (877-491-3463, www.rewardsnetwork.com) rebates your credit card for up to 15%of the cost of meals, beverages, tax, and tip. The network of restaurants operates nationwide, and membership is free.

PRIMECARD (800-444-8872, www.igtcard.com), a restaurant charge card, saves you up to 50% off meals and purchases at 1,000 restaurants and entertainment and retail establishments in New York, New Jersey, Connecticut, and south Florida.

ENTERTAINMENT

5. GO TO THE MUSEUM. Find out when your local museum(s) are free, and make it a habit to visit them then. Even better, ask your local library if it has museum passes. If so, you can go when you choose—either for free or at a greatly reduced price.

6. HEAD FOR THE THEATER. Become a patron of the arts by going to student shows. High schools and colleges offer wonderful productions and recitals that are free or low cost and that deserve your support. Ditto for regional theater productions, which might be a little more expensive but are still a great buy. You might see the next Tom Hanks and Meryl Streep before the rest of the world discovers them.

$ TIP Go local. Your high school or college baseball, hockey, football, soccer, and basketball games are far cheaper than their professional equivalents. Take your own lunch and snacks.

7. ENJOY THE MOVIES. Almost everything winds up being on DVD before long, but there's still something wonderful about seeing a great movie (or just an entertaining one) in a live theater surrounded by other moviegoers. You can make moviegoing a lot cheaper by using your AAA membership to purchase tickets online. Visit your club's Web site at www.aaa.com, and you'll find out how to save 25% by buying a four- or five-pack of tickets for some of the leading movie house chains.

$ TIP Some theaters reduce prices for films that start before 12 noon.

8. STAY AT HOME. During the Great Depression, parlor and board games became the rage—in 1935, Parker Brothers introduced Monopoly and had trouble keeping up with the demand, churning out 20,000 sets a week. If you think we watch too much TV and have become a nation of couch potatoes (or even if you don't think so), set aside time on the weekends or in the evenings to play Scrabble, Charades, Trivial Pursuit, and Clue with your family. Or combine parlor games with at-home potluck dinners with like-minded friends.

9. JOIN A BOOK CLUB. Drawing inspiration again from the people of the Great Depression, why not set up your own salon, discussion group, or book club? The golden age of the mystery novel came in the 1930s, when Americans devoured books by Agatha Christie, Dashiell Hammett, and Raymond Chandler. You could continue the tradition by reading mysteries, or perhaps have your club read all the books that won the Pulitzer or National Book Award.

Starting your own. Many people have been inspired by Oprah Winfrey's television book club and have started their own. There's excellent advice on how to do so at www.oprah. com. Local booksellers are usually happy to offer discounts to book groups.

You'll find that publishers often include guides for reading groups on their Web sites or at the end of the books themselves. And some authors are happy to schedule phone calls with groups that are reading their work. (Check individual publishers' Web sites to see details on author chats.)

Your local library may also sponsor a book group or help you start one. Chances are, you can gather enough copies for your group through interlibrary loan. Some library systems make it a snap by providing a "book club in a bag" with 10 copies of a title and background information on the book.

VACATIONS

One plus of a recession is that the price of vacations goes down. Hotels cut their rates or offer a second or third night for free or half price. Cruise lines give free airfare from your city to the departure dock. Packaged trips toss in extras. Even the legendary Queen Mary 2 offers up to 75% off its sailings, with many cruises well under $1,000. So there's no need to forgo getting away.

10. STAY CLOSE TO HOME. Do you live near a big city? Hotels that want to fill up rooms often offer weekend packages with discounted room rates, along with free breakfast or parking and passes to museums, sports events, and famous sites. To find these deals, check your local newspaper's weekend travel section or the convention and visitor's bureau Web site.

11. TAKE DAY TRIPS. Libraries, museums, historical societies, Ys, and religious congregations often sponsor day trips to fascinating places. Just getting away to new surroundings, usually on a comfortable motor coach, can be a wonderful break.

12. HEAD FOR THE HILLS. Visit a state or national park. Chances are, you live near one or the other. You can camp in the park or stay at inexpensive accommodations nearby. To find state parks, search online, typing in "state parks" and your state name, and go to www.nps.gov for national parks.

> **$ TIP** Other great yet inexpensive family vacation opportunities can be found on a farm stay. These are available around the country, but they are most abundant in Pennsylvania (888-856-6622) and Vermont (866-348-FARM, www.vtfarms.org). Most include at least breakfast and lots of outdoor chores and activities.

13. BOOK A PACKAGE. A deal that includes airfare, hotel, and, ideally, a rental car is almost always cheaper than putting the individual pieces together. Among the best packagers are

CIE Tours: 800-CIE-TOUR, www.cietours.com

Club ABC: 888-TOURS-ABC, www.clubabc.com

General Tours: 800-221-2216, www.generaltours.com

Maxxim Vacations: 800-567-6666, www.maxxim vacations.com

Mayflower Tours: 800-323-7604, www.mayflowertours.com

Overseas Adventure Tours: 800-493-6824, www.oat.com

Picasso Tours: 800-995-7997, www.picassotours.com

Ritz Tours: 888-345-7489, www.ritztours.com

TourCrafters: 800-621-2259, www.tourcrafters.com

Trafalgar Tours: 866-544-4434, www.trafalgartours.com

14. RIDE THE RAILS. Amtrak offers great rail and hotel packages around the United States and Canada. For details, contact Amtrak at 800-268-7252, www.amtrakvacations.com.

15. TRAVEL IN A GROUP. Most cruise lines and travel companies offer 20% off for groups of 20 or more. Some allow the person organizing a small group to travel or sail for free or for half off. Grand Circle Travel (800-959-0405, www.gct.com), for example, gives a free trip to the person who gathers together ten people for its river cruises, and Trafalgar Tours (866-544-4434, www.trafalgartours.com) offers a 5% discount for groups of five to eight. Be sure to ask about this whenever you're planning a trip.

16. FLY AS A COURIER. If you can leave home at the last minute and manage with only carry-on luggage, you can fly abroad for up to 85% off the usual fare if you go as a courier. Although you're delivering something for someone else, heavy lifting is not part of the deal. Couriers carry a list of the items that are being shipped under their name, but they typically never see the cargo. Your luggage allotment is given to the courier firm. International Association of Air Travel Couriers, 402-218-1982, www.courier.org.

17. BE A DANCER. Many cruise lines seek out gentlemen who are good dancers. In exchange for asking single women to dance and generally being nice to them, they get free accommodations (though the agencies that arrange the programs charge a small fee, such as $28 a day).

Similar programs exist for experts who can speak on topics ranging from geology and history to film and music. Art instructors and clergy are also sought for cruises. You receive no payment, but you (and often a companion) travel for free. Compass Speakers & Entertainment, 954-568-3801, www.com passspeakers.com.

THE HOLIDAYS

These tips apply to religious and national holidays as well as anniversaries, birthdays, and graduations.

18. SET UP A FAMILY AND FRIENDS GIFT EXCHANGE. Buying something for everyone in your family at holiday time can be awesome, and even a pain. Not only is it expensive, but it's very time-consuming, especially if you've got a Brady Bunch–type family. Instead, put all the names in a bowl and have each person draw just one. This not only cuts back on the cost and the stress of shopping, but also gives you more time to think about what to give that one special relative, roommate, or friend.

19. SHARE HOLIDAY DINNERS. It's a lot of work to shop, prepare, and serve Thanksgiving, Christmas, or Hanukkah meals. So make these potluck affairs, with everyone bringing part of the meal. (This works well for New Year's Eve, too.) Those who don't like to stuff the turkey or bake pies can bring the sparkling water, wine, or champagne. Or, assign them the cleanup detail.

20. GO WITH THE YEAR. Have everyone in the family agree that in 2009, they will spend only $20.09 on each gift. Boost that to $20.10 next year. Being a lighthearted Scrooge, especially for friends and relatives "who don't need another thing," puts the emphasis on creativity and cleverness rather than on how expensive a present is.

Carrying that theme further, get everyone in your group to agree to buy gifts only at yard sales or thrift shops.

As Aldous Huxley said, "Life [is] routine punctuated by little orgies," and we hope that this chapter has helped you find many little orgies that you can afford.

FOR FURTHER INFORMATION

OUTLET BOUND: GUIDE TO THE NATION'S BEST OUTLETS; www.outlet bound.com.

BOOK CLUB COMPANION: A COMPREHENSIVE GUIDE TO THE READING GROUP EXPERIENCE, by Diana Loevy (New York: Berkley, 2006).

Recession Punch

HOW TO SERVE 50 PEOPLE FOR UNDER $25

Now that you've finished this book and are armed with tips for winning personal victories during tough patches, it's time to celebrate. Invite friends over for a cup of Recession Punch. But in keeping with the new Age of Frugality, ask each of them to bring a bit of food.

The Punch

Boil gently for 5 minutes:
> *2 cups of sugar*
> *1 cup of water*

Add:
> *2 cups of concentrated fruit punch*
> *1 cup of lemonade*
> *2 cups of orange juice*
> *2 cups of pineapple juice*
> *2 bottles of inexpensive champagne-style wine*
> *2 quarts of ginger ale*
> *1 cup of club soda*

Note: You can use inexpensive champagne-style wine, as its flavor will be diluted. This punch can be served warm or cold, depending upon the season. Sparkling apple cider may be substituted for the perfect nonalcoholic alternative.

—An old family recipe

Index

A

AAA membership, 218
AARP, 161, 164, 204
Abbreviated budgets, 28
Account(s):
  checking, 97
  college, 146–147
  liquidity of, 129–130
  listing your, 2
  protection of, 14–16, 105
  REWARDChecking, 21–22, 24–25
  savings, 21, 55, 69
Account management, 113–133
  and Ponzi schemes, 125–131
  and recession-resistant industries,
    114–117
  and selling stocks, 121–125
  and stock-picking strategies, 117–121
Account statements, 98, 130
Adams, John, 78
Adjustable-rate loans, 78
Adjusted gross income (AGI), 211
ADV Form, 128
Advanced Placement courses, 146
Advisors, financial, 9, 126
AFL-CIO, 151, 179
AGI (adjusted gross income), 211
Aging, 47, 157–167
  benefits of, 164–166
  and employment, 158–164
Alternative funding (for college), 141–
  145
American Bar Association, 162

American Recovery and Reinvestment
  Act (stimulus package), 34–36, 62,
  81, 136, 177, 184
American Share Insurance (ASI), 21, 24
American Society of Appraisers, 5
Americorps, 147
Amtrak, 165, 221
Analysts, financial, 132
Anthem Blue Cross Blue Shield, 193
Appraiser Association of America, 5
Assessors, 88–90
Assets, 9–10
Assurant Health, 193
Athletic scholarships, 146
ATMs, 70, 97
Audit, personal (*see* Personal financial
  inventory)
"Audit ale," 2
Automatic withdrawals, 31, 98
Average national loan rates, 64

B

Background checks (on stockbrokers),
  128–129
Bankrate, Inc., 16, 19, 54, 99, 104
Bankruptcy, 83, 109, 124, 143, 154, 173
Bank(s):
  failed, 16–18
  insurance, 14–21
  [*see also* ccount(s)]
Barnum, Phineas Taylor, 27, 52
Bauer Financial, 18
Benefits, employee, 183

Bernie L. Madoff Investment Securities, 125
Beverage industry, 115
Bicycling, 34, 208
Big Y, 151
Bill payment, 28–31, 36, 99, 184
Bond ratings, 173
Book clubs, 218
Broker loan rate, 63
Brokerage accounts, 63
Brokers, real estate, 81
Budgeting, 27–49, 188
  and car insurance, 41–46
  and everyday expenses, 32–36
  and grocery costs, 37–40
  and homeowner's insurance, 41–42, 47–48
Buffett, Warren, 122
Burke, Billie, 157
Bush, George W., 14, 84
BuyandHold.com, 22

C
Capital One, 97
Car Care Council, 43
Car insurance, 41–46
Car rentals, 96–97
Career counselors, 158–159, 162
Career Guide to Industries, 159
Cash:
  as gift, 71
  paying with, 38, 98
  running out of, 51–52 (*See also* Loans)
Cavanagh, Walter, 96
CDARS Program, 16
Celtic Insurance, 193
Certificates of deposit (CDs), 16, 19, 22, 55, 188
Check Retirement Jobs.com, 161–162
Checking accounts, 97
Christie, Agatha, 13, 20
Church health plans, 186
Clearinghouses, 130
COBRA, 184–186, 193
Collateral, 55–56, 63
Collection agencies, 106

College accounts, 146–147
College Board, 136–138, 144
College expenses, 135–155
  alternative funding for, 141–145
  and family members/friends, 151–152
  high school preparation for, 137–141
  and parents, 149–151
  paying back, 152–154
  and students, 146–148
  tuition-free schools, 149
Collision coverage, 42
Commercial loans, 54–56
Common bond guidelines, 23
Community Bank, 20
Community colleges, 147
Company loans, 57–58
Compass Speakers & Entertainment, 222
Concert discounts, 165
Confucius, 197–198
Consolidation, debt, 102
Consumers Union, 105
Conversion fees, 97
Coogan, Jackie, 198
Cool Savings, 40
Cosigners, 86, 145
Counselors:
  career, 158–159
  guidance, 137, 140–141
Coupons, 37–38
Couriers, 221
Coverdell Education Savings Account (ESA), 151
Craigs List, 198
Credit card(s), 31, 95–112
  debit cards vs., 104–106
  and debt negotiation, 106–108
  and home equity loans, 103–104
  interest rates on, 101–103
  payments on, 99–101
  recession-proofing your, 96–98
  and your credit score, 108–111
Credit scores, 87, 108–111
  and car insurance, 45
  and PLUS loans, 143
Credit Union National Association (CUNA), 24

Credit unions, 23–24
Creditors, 32
Croesus, 67–68
Cruises, 222

D

Dancing, 160, 222
Database of State Incentives for
    Renewable Energy, 36
Debit cards, credit cards vs., 104–106
Debt negotiation, 106–108
Deductibles:
    on car insurance, 42
    on homeowner's insurance, 47
Default rates, 99–100
Dining choices, 33–34, 216–217
Dinkytown, 100, 103
Direct deposit, 72
Direct Mail Association, 35
Discount(s):
    on car insurance, 43–44
    codes (for online shopping), 36
    dining programs, 33, 216–217
Diversification, portfolio, 115, 126
Dividend-paying stocks, 22, 70,
    117
Dollar cost averaging, 118
Dow Jones Industrial Average, 118,
    126
Drug industry, 115

E

Eating in, eating out vs., 216
EBay, 64
Economic hardship deferment, 153
EDGAR, 119
eHealthInsurance, 193–194
Electronic payments, 98, 100
Emergency Economic Stabilization Act
    of 2008, 14
Employee benefits, 183
Employment (see Finding work)
Energy, 35, 41
Energy Star, 41
Entertainment, 217–219
Equal Employment Opportunity
    Commission, 163

Equifax, 108, 110
Exit interviews, 183
Expenses, 29–30, 48
Experian, 108
Extended repayment, 152

F

FAFSA (see Free Application for
    Federal Student Aid)
Fair Isaac Corporation (FICO), 143,
    145 (See also Credit scores)
Farm stays, 220
"Fats" Domino, 135
Federal Deposit Insurance Corporation
    (FDIC), 10, 14–22, 24
Federal Housing Administration
    (FHA), 82, 85–86
Federal Reserve Board, 63
Federal Student Aid Information
    Center, 141
Federal Trade Commission (FTC), 58,
    106–107
FICO (see Fair Isaac Corporation)
Filene, Edward, 23
FinAid, 142, 152, 153
Financial advisors, 9, 126
Financial aid, 138–141
Financial analysts, 132
Financial hardship withdrawals, 59–60
Financial Industry Regulator Authority
    (FINRA), 129
Financial inventory, personal (see
    Personal financial inventory)
Finding work, 197–213
    and aging, 158–164
    interviews, 207–210
    tax deductions on, 210–212
    tips for, 198–204
    top employers, 205–206
"Fired" (see Losing your job)
Five O'Clock Club, 158–159
529 savings plans, state-sponsored, 150
Fixed-rate loans, 79
Flagstar Bank, 22
Flexible Executives, 204
Flexible spending accounts, 73, 182
Food industry, 115

Foreclosures, 77–87, 143
  and outside assistance, 82–83
  and refinancing, 84–87
  and short sales, 83–84
  and your lender, 79–82
Form ADV, 128
Fortune, 205
Foundation for Consumer Credit, 107
401(k) plans
  loans from, 59–61, 144
  and losing your job, 189–193
Freddie Mac, 83
Free Application for Federal Student
  Aid (FAFSA), 140, 142
FTC (*see* Federal Trade Commission)
Funds:
  hedge, 129
  money market, 20–22, 188
  mutual, 2–3, 20–21, 25–26, 122, 130

G
Gains, stock, 125
Gaming winnings, 71
Gardening industry, 116
Gift exchange, 222
GMAC, 46
Goldwyn, Samuel, 53
Goodyear, Charles, 52
Graduated repayment, 152
Grand Circle Travel, 221
Grandparents, and college costs, 151–152
Grants, 138–139, 146
Great Depression, 218
Green companies, 207–208
Greyhound, 165
Grocery costs, 37–40
Grocery Game, 40
Gross misconduct, 186
Group travel, 221
Growth, income vs., 114, 122
Guidance counselors, 137, 140–141
Guinness Book of World Records, 96

H
Harvard University, 135
Health care industry, 116, 160, 199

Health insurance, 183–186, 193–194
Heating cost assistance, 36
Hedge funds, 129
High school, and college preparation,
  137–141
Holidays, 222–223
Home equity line of credit (HELOC),
  57
Home equity loans, 56, 103–104,
  143–144
Home Ownership Preservation
  Foundation (HOPE), 80, 82
Home-based businesses, 163
Homeowner's insurance, 41–42, 47–48
Hope Credit, 150
Hormel Foods, 116
Hotels, 96–97, 160, 165
Household inventory, 4
Household products industry, 116
Hubbard, Frank McKinney, 67
HUD (*see* U.S. Department of Housing
  and Urban Development)
Human resources departments, 183
Hundred Years' War, 52
Hurricane Katrina, 7
Huxley, Aldous, 223

I
Income, growth vs., 114, 122
Income-contingent repayment, 153
Individual retirement accounts (IRAs)
  loans from, 61–62, 144
  rollovers, 189–191
INGdirect, 21
Insurance
  car, 41–46
  health, 183–186, 193–194
  homeowner's, 4, 41–42, 47–48
  life, 8, 62–63, 183
  reimbursements from, 70
  unemployment, 174–178, 183
Interest rates:
  on commercial loans, 55
  on credit cards, 101–103
  on PLUS loans, 145
Internal Revenue Service (IRS), 62,
  123–125, 154, 191, 211

International Association of Air Travel
    Couriers, 221
Internet, 130
Internet banks, 14
Interviews:
    exit, 183
    job, 162–163, 207–210
IRAs (*see* Individual retirement
    accounts)
IRS (*see* Internal Revenue Service)

J

JLBG Health, 193
Job(s):
    finding a (*see* Finding work)
    part-time, 197–198
    seasonal, 200–201
    suitable, 178
Job interviews, 162–163, 207–210, 212
Job loss (*see* Losing your job)

K

Kelley Blue Book, 5
Kelly Services, 203–204
King and I, The, 202

L

Laddering, 19
Lancaster, Hal, 169
Layoffs (*see* Losing your job)
Lehman Brothers, 20
Letters of reference, 183
Liabilities, 7
Libraries, 29, 120–121, 210, 217,
    219
Life insurance, 8, 62–63, 183
Lifetime Learning Credit, 150
LIHEAP (Low-Income Home Energy
    Assistance Program), 36
Liquidity (of accounts), 129–130
Living trusts, 15
Living wills, 8
Loans, 53–64
    adjustable-rate, 78
    college, 138–139, 152–154
    commercial, 54–56
    company, 57–58

fixed-rate, 79
401(k), 59–61
home equity, 56, 103–104, 143–144
IRA, 61–62
from life insurance, 62–63
margin account, 63
payday, 58
personal, 53–54
real estate, 56–57
secured vs. unsecured, 53
Local businesses, 199
Local scholarships, 141
Losing your job, 169–179, 181–195
    preventative measures, 170–171,
        173–174
    steps to take after, 182–189
    and temporary health insurance,
        193–194
    and unemployment insurance, 174–178
    warning signs of, 171–173
    and your 401(k), 189–193
Losses, stock, 124–125
Low-Income Home Energy Assistance
    Program (LIHEAP), 36
Lump sum(s):
    severance packages as, 189
    taking 401(k) plan as, 192

M

Mackay, Harvey, 181
Madoff, Bernie, 125–126, 129–130
Manpower, 203
Margin account loans, 63
Margin calls, 63
Medicare, 184
Metro-Goldwyn-Mayer, 53
Microsoft Money, 4, 28
Mint.com, 4
Mom Corps, 204
Money market funds, 20–22, 188
Moody's, 173, 189
Mortgage Bankers Association, 82
Mortgage Forgiveness Debt Relief Act,
    84
Mortgage lenders, 79–82, 84–85
Moses, Grandma, 158
Mothers (working), 204, 206

Movie discounts, 165, 218
MS EDIE, 15–16
Museums, 201, 217
Mutual funds, 2–3, 20–21, 122, 130

N
Nabisco, 115
National Assistance Referral (NEAR), 36
National Association of Health Underwriters, 185
National Association of Unclaimed Property Administration (NAUPA), 10
National Board for Certified Counselors, Inc., 159
National Credit Union Administration (NCUA), 21, 24
National Employment Lawyer Association, 186
National Foundation for Consumer Credit, 107
National Park Service, 166
Net worth, 4–7
North American Securities Association, 128

O
Obama, Barack, 34
Occupational Outlook Handbook, 159
Operation ABLE, 162
Outlook (weekly publication), 121
Overtime, 183

P
Parents, and college costs, 149–151
Parks, 166, 220
Part-time jobs, 197–198
Pasteur, Louis, 77
Pay-As-You-Drive (PAYD) insurance, 46
Payday loans, 58
Payroll deduction plans, 72
Penalty rates, 99
Perkins loans, 138–139, 152
Personal financial inventory, 1–11
    household assets in, 4

and net worth, 4–7
and stockbrokers/advisors, 9
and unclaimed assets, 9–10
Personal loans, 53–54
Phone plans, 34–35
PLUS loans, 143, 145
Ponzi schemes, 125–131
Portfolios:
    diversification of, 115, 126
    laddered, 19
Post 9/11 GI Bill, 148
Potlucks, 216, 222–223
Power of attorney, 8
Primecard, 33, 217
Private loans, 143, 145
Profit-sharing plans, 73
Progressive Insurance, 42, 46
Promissory notes, 53
Promotional interest rates, 103
Property taxes, 87–94
    comparing homes to appeal, 90–91
    exceptions that reduce, 93
    formal hearings on, 92
    small mistakes on, 88–90
Protecting your money, 13–26
    in bank accounts, 14–16, 105
    in credit unions, 23–24
    and the FDIC, 16–19
    money market funds, 20–22
    in smaller banks, 24–25
Public transit, 34, 166
Pyramid schemes, 125–131

Q
Quicken, 4, 28

R
Real estate brokers, 81
Real estate loans, 56–57
Recession punch, 225–226
Recession-resistant industries, 114–117
Reference letters, 183
Referrals (for financial advisors), 126
Refinancing, 84–87
Registered representatives, 128–129
Registration (of firms), 127–128
Renting your house, 82–83

Repayment types (of college loans), 152–153
Required appeals procedure, 88
Reserve Officers' Training Corps (ROTC), 148
Reserve Primary Money Market Fund, 20
Restaurants, 216–217
Retirement savings, 59–62, 144, 150, 189–193
RetirementJobs.com, 199, 204
REWARDChecking accounts, 21–22, 24–25
Rewards Network, 33, 217
Rogers, Will, 136, 215
Roosevelt, Theodore, 158
ROTC, 148
"Rule of 72," 74

S
Safe deposit box, 3–4, 7–8
Safe harbors (*see* Protecting your money)
Sallie Mae, 138
Saving money (frugality), 215–223
  dining choices, 216–217
  entertainment, 217–219
  holidays, 222–223
  vacations, 219–222
Savings accounts, 21, 55, 69
Savings bonds, 3
  Series EE, 71–72, 151
  series I, 22, 72
Savings strategies, 67–74
  personal, 68–69
  work-related, 71–73
Scholarships, 151
  athletic, 146
  local, 138, 141
Seasonal jobs, 200–201
Second mortgages, 56
Secured loans, 53
Securities and Exchange Commission (SEC), 21, 119, 127–128
Securities Investor Protection Corporation (SIPC), 131
Security systems, 47

Selling stocks, 121–125
Senior discounts, 164–166
Serial numbers, 4
Severance packages, 147, 183, 186, 188–189
Shakespeare, William, 51, 95
Shopping lists, 37
Short sales, 83–84
Short Term Medical Insurance, 194
Short-term health insurance, 193–194
Sick pay, 183
Simple Tuition, 145
SIPC (Securities Investor Protection Corporation), 131
Smaller banks, 24–25, 85
SmartExchange Program, 3
SMARTHINKING, 202
Smoking, 32, 47
Sons of Liberty, 77–78
Stafford loans, 138–139, 142–143, 152
Standard & Poor's, 22, 117, 121, 126, 173, 189
Statements, account, 98, 130
State-sponsored 529 savings plans, 150
Stimulus package (*see* American Recovery and Reinvestment Act)
Stock(s), 9
  dividend-paying, 22, 70
  purchase plans, 72
  recession-resistant, 114–117
  selection strategies, 117–121
  utility, 22
  selling strategies, 121–124
  worthless, 123–124
Stockbrokers, 9
  background checks on, 128–129
  and margin account loans, 63
Stop-loss orders, 9, 122–123
Store brands, 39
Stout, Rex, 158
Students, and college costs, 146–148
Suitable jobs, 178
Summer classes, 147
SunTrust Bank, 18
Sutton, Willie, 13–14

T

Tax deductions:
  job-search related, 210–212
  for private vs. PLUS loans, 145
  for student loans, 154
Tax refunds, 35–36, 70
Taxes, property (*see* Property taxes)
TEACH grant program, 147
Temp agencies, 203
Temporary health insurance, 193–194
10 til 2 (company), 204
Theater productions, 217
Thoreau, Henry David, 27–28, 30
Top employers, 205–206
Trafalgar Tours, 221
Trailways, 166
TransUnion, 108, 110
Travel industry, 161
Treasury Hunt Web site, 10
TreasuryDirect program, 3, 72
Trustee-to-trustee rollovers, 190–191
Tucker, Sophie, 113
Tuition (*see* College expenses)
Tuition payment plans, 142
Tuition-free schools, 149
Turner, Ted, 181
Tusser, Thomas, 1
Tutor.com, 202–203
Tutoring, 160, 202–203
TutorVista.com, 203
Twain, Mark, 52

U

Unclaimed assets, 9–10
Unemployment (*see* Losing your job)
Unemployment insurance, 174–178,
  183
United Health One, 193
Universal default penalty, 99
Unsecured loans, 53

U.S. Bureau of Labor, 159
U.S. Department of Education, 139
U.S. Department of Energy, 35
U.S. Department of Housing and
  Urban Development (HUD),
  79–80, 82
U.S. Department of Labor, 178
U.S. Department of Veterans Affairs, 148
U.S. Government Fund (Community
  Bank), 20
U.S. government Web sites, 10
U.S. Treasury Department, 21
USAA, 43
Utilities industry, 116
Utility stocks, 22

V

Vacations, 183, 219–222
Value Line Investment Survey, 22, 119–
  121
Variable expenses, 29–30
Veribanc, 18
Veterans Administration, 82
Veterans' Benefits Improvement Act, 82
Volunteer work, 204

W

Walden (Henry David Thoreau), 27–28
Want ads, 198
Waste disposal industry, 117
We Got Fired! (Harvey Mackay), 181
Whistler, James Abbott McNeill, 52
Whiteface Mountain, 166
Wikipedia, 198
Wills, 8
Winfrey, Oprah, 219
Work, finding (*see* Finding work)
Work reviews, 172
Work-study awards, 139
Worthless stocks, 123–124

About the Author

Nancy Dunnan has been writing about the world of finance for more than 20 years. She appears regularly on CNN, Business News Network, Bloomberg Radio, and National Public Radio in New York City. In addition to *Recession-Proof Your Life,* she is the author of *$50–$5,000, Dunnan's Guide to Your Investments, Never Call Your Broker on Monday, Never Balance Your Checkbook on Tuesday,* and *Never Short a Stock on Wednesday.* She also writes monthly columns for *Bottom Line Retirement,* www.Buyandhold.com, www.TheOnlineInvestor.com, and www.HomeAdvisor.msn.com.

Nancy was awarded the Distinguished Service Award in Investment Education from the Investment Education Institute, an affiliate of the National Association of Investors Corp. A native of Fort Dodge, Iowa, and with degrees from Simmons College and Case Western Reserve University, she lives in Manhattan—on a budget, of course.